ROOTS THAT REFRESH

ROOTS THAT REFRESH

A Celebration
of Reformation Spirituality

Alister McGrath

Hodder & Stoughton
LONDON SYDNEY AUCKLAND

The quotation from 'Little Gidding', from *Four Quartets* by T.S. Eliot, is reproduced
with permission from Faber & Faber Ltd, and Harcourt Brace Jovanovich, Inc.
© 1943 by T.S. Eliot and renewed 1971 by Esme Valerie Eliot.

British Library Cataloguing in Publication Data
Cataloguing in Publication Data is available from The British Library

ISBN 0-340-55803-2

Copyright © 1991 by Alister McGrath.

First published in Great Britain 1992.

Published by Hodder & Stoughton,
a division of Hodder and Stoughton Ltd,
Mill Road, Dunton Green, Sevenoaks, Kent TN13 2YA.
Editorial Office: 47 Bedford Square, London WC1B 3DP.

Photoset by Chippendale Type Ltd., Otley, West Yorkshire.

Printed in Great Britain by Clays Ltd., St. Ives plc

Contents

Preface

I remember how, as a small boy, one of my greatest pleasures was rummaging through my grandparents' attic. For me, the room was something of a treasure house, full of books, paintings and household items dating back to the first decades of the twentieth century. Situated at the top of a rambling Victorian house, this room had long served as a repository for all kinds of items which, although old, nobody had the heart to throw away. 'They might come in useful some time' was the homespun philosophy which lay beneath this reluctance to discard anything of potential value or use.

I have since come to discover that this same attitude underlies the best in Christian thinking. Responsible Christian theology and spirituality regard the ideas and values of the past, not as obsolete, but as items with a potential continued distinguished history of use. This is especially the case with the spirituality of the Reformation, which may justly claim to lay the foundations of classic Evangelical spirituality. The idea of 'the classic' is complex, embracing a number of key ideas. A classic is a point of reference, a perennial resource, something whose meaning and relevance is not exhausted by and in its own day and age, but is available to others. Shakespeare's *Macbeth*, Beethoven's third symphony and Plato's *Republic* are all examples of classics which continue to find relevance and use in the modern period. Many modern writings will find service for at best a generation or two; a classic goes on, to find service among generations yet unborn. Reformation spirituality is a classic resource – a vital point of reference for modern Evangelicalism, as it seeks to clarify its self-understanding, and a continuing resource for the modern church, as it seeks to bring every resource at its disposal to bear on the needs of its situation.

The Reformation, like many other formative periods in Christian history, has much to offer us today. Works such as Jürgen Moltmann's *The Crucified God* (which is a superb contemporary exposition of Luther's theology of the cross) have brought home to us the considerable potential of the theology of the Reformation period; that recognition has yet to be extended to its spirituality. Yet the Reformation did more than lay the foundations of classic Evangelical spirituality; it opened up new and invigorating approaches to the Christian life, like a breath of fresh air in a smoke-filled room. The Reformation offers us an invitation to return to consider our scriptural roots, in order that we may turn once more, refreshed, to our own situation.

The spirituality of the Reformation is a living option for the modern church, concerned on the one hand to remain faithful to Scripture, and on the other to engage with the realities of modern life. For classic Evangelical spirituality represents more than a return to Scripture. It represents a systematic and coherent approach, by which the totality of the scriptural witness to the real and redemptive action of God through Christ could be focused upon and channelled into the everyday world. Scripture was not merely read and respected; it was recognised as possessing a relevance for every facet of Christian life. For the theologians of the Reformation did not develop their approaches to the spiritual life in the splendid isolation of monasteries or the ivory towers of the universities. These new approaches to the Christian life were forged and tested in the white heat of the crucibles of the great cities of early modern Europe. This classic Evangelical spirituality has been tried and tested – and yet is now neglected.

The present work is a small and very modest contribution towards recovering this classic approach to Christian spirituality. As more and more Christian churches within the Protestant tradition decide to return to their Evangelical roots for spiritual refreshment, this book aims to make available some of the riches of that tradition to its modern heirs. If a return to one's spiritual roots is a precondition for growth and development, as many recent surveys of modern American religious life suggest to be the case, then it is essential that the spirituality of the Reformation should be made available and accessible to those who wish to pursue and benefit from the classic approaches to Evangelical spirituality which seem to have gained a new credibility and vitality in recent years.

This work offers a modest reading of recovery, making these ideas intelligible and accessible to the present. It is a small and limited exercise in allowing the modern period to overhear the conversations of another era on the theme of spirituality. This is not a matter of unthinking regression to the past, but of a critical and appreciative dialogue with a genuinely creative and interesting moment in Christian history. For modern Evangelicals to study the Reformation is not only to rediscover what we have forgotten and repressed, but to learn something about how we might put our fragmented world back together again. It is also to be prepared to be *surprised* by the reformers, to discover how much the Reformation differs from its commonly accepted stereotypes.

The stimulus to write this book came when I was invited to deliver the 1990 Ezra Squier Tipple Lectures at Drew University, Madison, New Jersey, to an audience of clergy, seminarians and laity drawn largely from the Greater New England area, on the theme of 'Reformation Spirituality'.* This invitation offered me the opportunity to explain the nature and relevance of the spirituality of the Reformation, and explore these ideas with an audience who firmly intended to *use* them in their pastoral ministry. The considerable warmth and enthusiasm with which these lectures were received convinced me of the importance of making this spirituality available to as wide an audience as possible.

I am grateful to Professor Thomas Ogletree (now Dean of Yale

* The four original lectures are published in the Spring 1991 number of *The Gateway* (the journal of Drew University Theological School), vol. 60, no.2. Material drawn from those lectures is here reproduced with kind permission of the editors.

Divinity School) for the invitation to deliver the 1990 Tipple lectures, and to Bishop James Ault and the faculty of Drew University for their hospitality. I have also included related material drawn from public lectures given at Princeton Theological Seminary and the Memorial Church, Harvard University around the same time. The material was rewritten for presentation at a conference of Christians United for Reformation (CURE) held at the First Presbyterian Church, Hollywood, California, in the spring of 1991. I am grateful for the many helpful comments I received there, and to Michael Horton for his hospitality. I guess that if these ideas can work in Hollywood, they can work just about anywhere.

Finally, a word about citations from the works of the reformers. I have made my own translations from the original sixteenth-century Latin, German and French, in an attempt to convey the freshness of the originals. At points, however, I have had to interpret or paraphrase terms and ideas which would be unfamiliar to modern readers. No distortion of the meaning of the texts has resulted, to the best of my belief. After much thought, I have decided not to give references for citations. They are not necessary in a work of this nature, which has no pretensions to being scholarly.

One day, I hope to write the volumes that a full academic presentation of these reflections would require. A full account of the spirituality of this remarkably dynamic and creative period in Christian history would include the rich and valuable contributions of Catholic Evangelicalism, making use of the works of individuals such as Marguerite of Navarre and Gasparo Contarini. It would draw upon the resources of the English Reformation, not least its considerable contributions to the prayers and liturgy of the Christian tradition. And it would attempt to encompass the sumptuous heritage of those reformers throughout Europe whom history has chosen to describe as 'minor', yet who include among their numbers some of the finest writers and thinkers of their day. When I finally get round to writing the academic work which is at present but a dream, it will provide detailed documentation for all references and citations. For the moment, this work must suffice.

But I have already apologised enough for the limitations placed upon this work. Our theme awaits us.

1   Light after the
Shadows: The Vitality of
Reformation Spirituality

Light is a symbol of hope. In the late summer of 1914, it seemed to many Europeans that this light was about to be extinguished as its greatest nations stood poised on the brink of war. Viscount Grey, then British Foreign Secretary, captured this sombre mood as he stood looking out of his windows upon London's Whitehall on 3 August 1914, and reflected upon the implications of that summer's grim events. 'The lamps are going out all over Europe. We shall not see them lit again in our lifetime.' A light flickering, finally to go out, symbolised the end of an era of hope as the shadows lengthened before the darkness.

Precisely the opposite sentiment prevailed four hundred years earlier. In the year 1535, after many years of struggle for independence, the city of Geneva finally gained its freedom from the powerful Duchy of Savoy. The newly independent city decided to make a break with both the political and the religious past, and align itself with a major new religious force now sweeping through Europe – the Reformation. During the following year, John Calvin would arrive to give Genevan Evangelicalism a much-needed sense of direction and purpose. As early as 1535, however, the city council decided to signal its decision to align itself with the forces of the future. It chose a motto for the city which would henceforth resonate throughout history: *post tenebras lux* – after the shadows, light! A new era of hope seemed to have dawned.

11

Geneva's decision to adopt the Reformation followed a pattern set by the majority of the great cities of northern Europe. Yet it was more than a new political order that was dawning in the cities of Europe at this time; a new Christian spirituality was being created and developed, faithful to Scripture and deeply rooted in the Christian tradition on the one hand, yet capable of meeting the needs and opportunities of the modern age and its cities on the other. It is this spirituality which is the subject of the present book.

To study the spirituality of the Reformation is not to luxuriate in romanticism. It is not to look back in nostalgia, like some old-timer hankering after the good old days when everything was better than it is now. It is not like the sentimental scrutiny of sepia-tinted photographs, nor the wistful recollection of days of lost innocence, a longing for a bygone period and its security. Rather, it is a hard-headed examination of past events, individuals and ideas, with a view to exploiting their present potential. It is to reach into our Christian past, and recover some of its riches. It is a critical awareness that not everything in the Christian present is quite what it could be, linked with a willingness to consider alternative possibilities – an attitude with a distinguished history of use within the Christian tradition. The Reformation witnessed the birth of classic Evangelical spirituality; the modern period needs to know about and benefit from it.

A Spirituality for the Modern Age

Historians find it convenient to give names to periods of history. The Reformation is generally agreed to stand at the dawn of the 'early modern period'. Time and time again, the Reformation marks the junction of the medieval and modern eras. It represents a parting of the ways – the dying world of the Middle Ages, and the emerging world of modernity. Many religious, social, political and economic developments which we take for granted in the modern world owe their origins to the European Reformation. Equally, of course, there many important developments which took place much later than the sixteenth century, tracing their origins to the Enlightenment or the French Revolution. The Reformation does not anticipate each and every aspect of modern life.

Nevertheless, there are important and vital points at which the Reformation makes contact with our modern situation. Time after time, the reformers are seen to link in with concerns, anxieties and aspirations which we can recognise as being our own. At point after point, there is a surprisingly contemporary feel to the writings of the period. Historically, this is precisely what we should expect. The Reformation had to develop forms of Christian thought and action capable of relating to the new age which dawned with the collapse of the Middle Ages. Medieval forms of spirituality were, in general, simply not capable of relating to the new needs and concerns of the modern world. They had to be replaced. The Reformation may be regarded as a necessary, and perhaps an overdue, attempt to relate the gospel to the new world of the cities, in which the laity were increasingly playing a dominant role.

In that seminal aspects of modern western society trace their origins to Europe at this time, it is to be expected that Reformation spirituality – developed with the needs of this new social order in mind – should prove capable of relating directly to our own day and age. Modern western society may have moved on far from its origins in sixteenth-century Europe – but time after time, the connections are seen to remain. To study Reformation spirituality is to study forms of spirituality which still connect up with the social, personal and existential concerns of modern western humanity. That they do not link up with every aspect of modern life is only to be expected; history has, after all, moved on. But vital connections remain, awaiting discovery and use by the believers of today.

Caricatures die hard, and perhaps one of the most influential caricatures of Christian history lies in the nineteenth-century suggestion that the Reformation and its inheritance were devoid of any spirituality. The very phrase 'Reformation spirituality' was alleged to be an oxymoron, a blatant self-contradiction. It is a pleasure to be able to write this book in the knowledge that this crude stereotype is in what one hopes to be irreversible decline.

Recent scholarship has revealed many of the leading figures of the Reformation as individuals with a passionate concern for the pastoral, spiritual and social well-being of their people – men who were concerned to ground their theologies firmly in the usually humdrum, yet occasionally terrifying, realities of everyday life. Their search for an authentically Christian spirituality was grounded in their belief that true knowledge of God was transformative, capable of deeply changing the mental, experiential and social worlds of those who grasped it. In undertaking that same quest for a renewed and authentic Christian spirituality today, we could do far worse than engage in dialogue with such figures as Luther and Calvin.

Furthermore, recent scholarship has largely discarded the obsolete polemics of earlier periods. For example, Roman Catholic writers are increasingly viewing the reformers as writers and preachers concerned with the creative restatement and application of the Christian faith in a period of exceptional difficulty and instability. There is growing sympathy for the suggestion that it was not so much the reformers, but rather political and social currents in the late Renaissance, which split the medieval church asunder, destroying its unity. The rise of nationalism and increasing trends towards political absolutism in Europe are among the more obvious currents of this type. Indeed, it is possible to argue that the Reformation provided a vital check upon the scope of such developments, by preventing the secularisation of the church being extended to the secularisation of the Christian faith itself.

There is now an increasing willingness on all sides to regard the reformers as individuals who were passionately and responsibly committed to the well-being of the church; as people who were obliged to break with the church of their day not because their ideas were heretical, but on account of the obstinacy of the late medieval church. The old wineskins could not cope with this potent new wine. With the welcome benefit of hindsight, we are increasingly viewing the reformers as individuals who developed new ideas and reclaimed old ideas which the church desperately needed to hear and act upon if it was to meet the new challenges and opportunities of the period.

That the Reformation ended up dividing the Christian church is a fact of history; it is equally a fact of history that the reformers did not intend this to take place, and took no pleasure in seeing it happen. One of the greatest tragedies of the sixteenth century is that individuals and groups, possessed of a vision to renew and revitalise the church *from within*, were forced out of that church largely, it seems, by sheer intransigence and a lack of vision on the part of its leaders. The distinguished Luther scholar Heinrich Bornkamm has brilliantly described the dilemma in which Luther found himself, as his pleas for renewal of the church seemed to fall on deaf ears:

> Luther was excluded from his church because of his criticism of the theology and the ecclesiastical conditions of his time. It was *his* church from which he was excluded, for it was for no other church that he uttered his fervent pleadings and prayers, and his painful laments and angry indictments. Everything he did and said and wrote was not against it, but for it, for its sake, not in order to establish a new church. It was because *his* church, the Roman church of that time, excluded him that an inner reform, which had often taken place before, became something new, outside of the existing church.

The Reformation, which was primarily conceived as a renewal of the church from within, thus ended up becoming something significantly different.

Recognition of this point goes some way towards explaining why there is currently renewed interest in and sympathy towards Evangelical spirituality within the modern Roman Catholic church. To make use of this classical Evangelical spirituality does not necessarily entail ceasing to be a Roman Catholic. The early sixteenth century bears witness to countless individuals within the Catholic church in Italy, Spain and France who adopted Evangelical spiritualities, yet remained within the Catholic church – often in very senior positions. Polarisation of the situation made it impossible to be both a Catholic and an Evangelical, forcing those unfortunate Catholic Evangelicals to make some very difficult decisions. But those days are firmly behind us. There is every indication that Evangelicalism is becoming increasingly acceptable and influential within the modern Roman Catholic church, recognised as a legitimate, workable and exciting option for the modern church. This need not be seen as an abandoning of Catholicism; rather, it should be seen as an overdue reclaiming of a classic form of Christian spirituality which the political atmosphere of the sixteenth century made a practical impossibility for Catholics. Evangelical spirituality is not divisive; it only became so on account of the power politics of a bygone age.

As his writings of the period 1513–19 make abundantly clear, Luther had no intention of founding a separate church. He had no thought of founding 'Lutheranism' as a body apart from the universal body of Christ. His aspiration was to recall the one church, of which he was a member, to renew its Christian vision and vocation from within. The idea of anyone calling themselves 'Lutheran' was anathema to him.

> I haven't been crucified for anyone! . . . How can I – poor, wretched corpse that I am – come to allow people to call the children of Christ by a name derived from my worthless name? No! No! No! My dear friends, let us call ourselves Christians, after the one whose teachings we hold fast to.

Reformation spirituality is nothing other than *Christian* spirituality, forged into new forms appropriate for the needs of the new age then dawning in western culture.

This reforging was urgently needed, if Christianity was to continue as a living option in modern Europe. During the Middle Ages, it had become as increasingly isolated from ordinary people as it had become increasingly firmly wedded to the fading medieval world. Ernst Curtius is one of the many scholars who have emphasised that it is a conveniently neglected matter of historical fact that much of what we refer to as 'medieval Christianity' or 'medieval spirituality' is actually *virtually totally monastic in its character and origins*. Sadly, historical realism dictates that we recognise that these medieval forms of spirituality had a strictly limited impact outside the monasteries – even

upon the clergy. The everyday life of the laity was often left virtually totally untouched by the spiritual riches being developed
behind monastic walls. Monastic spirituality was fashioned with
the monastic situation in mind, envisaging a lifestyle and outlook
quite alien to lay people. With the Reformation, the formative
centres of spirituality gradually shifted from the monasteries to
the market place, as the great cities of Europe became the
cradle and crucible of new ways of Christian thinking and acting.
Spirituality was not merely brought to the people; new forms of
the spiritual life were created, with their needs and situations
firmly in view.

Mirrored in this shift may be seen the political, social,
economic and religious changes which lie at the heart of
the formation of modern western culture. From its outset,
Reformation spirituality represented ideas with a future, possessing a high coefficient of relevance to the emerging needs
of modern western society. The waning of the Middle Ages
inevitably entailed a diminishing of the potential of medieval
forms of spirituality, which were generally linked with specifically
medieval ideas and institutions. With the birth of the new era in
human history which historians now designate the 'early modern
period', it was essential that new ways of conceiving and acting
out the Christian life should develop, unless Christianity were
to be seen as moribund, linked to the dying world of the Middle
Ages. The old religion was simply not capable of coping with the
unprecedented pressures and challenges of the new age.

The Reformation represented a sustained attempt to relate
the Christian faith to the conditions and lifestyles of this new
era. The spirituality of the Reformation was so deeply rooted
in the Christian tradition that it can justly be described as
'classic' – yet it was sufficiently responsive to the new situations
then developing that it can equally be described as 'modern'.
Mingling the classic and the modern, the Reformation is thus
well placed to address the needs of our own day and age,
where a consciousness of modernity is often tempered with
an awareness of the need for stability and continuity with the
past – a point which merits consideration in more detail.

Recovering a Sense of Christian Identity

The Reformation was fundamentally a quest for Christian identity and authenticity. It represents one of those great and rare moments in Christian history, when the church was prepared to re-examine itself. It was prepared to face up to a series of deeply disturbing questions concerning its role and its relevance. The Christian church has always been prone to a form of inertia. By that, I do not mean that it stands still, immovable amidst the changing situations in which it finds itself. Rather, I mean that there is a certain inbuilt tendency to suppose that anything that happens in the life and thought of the church is invariably a good thing. There is an assumption that 'the way things are' is the same as 'the way things are meant to be'. It is a *laissez-faire* approach to Christianity. There is inertia, in the sense that there is a reluctance to adopt a *critical* attitude towards the way things are, apparently on the basis of the assumption that what has happened is somehow *meant* to have happened. There is a reluctance to interrogate development, to challenge change.

And it is here that the Reformation had a fundamental contribution to make – a contribution which is continued in what has come to be known as 'the Protestant principle'. One of the deepest and most powerful wellheads which nourished the Reformation and its heritage is a spirit of creative protest, of prophetic criticism. This springs from the recognition of the sovereignty of God over his creation and his church, and of the living character of his revelation of himself in Jesus Christ and through Scripture. This creative and critical principle is grounded in a dynamic understanding of God's self-revelation, and his call to the Christian church to re-examine and renew itself in the light of this. Classical Evangelical spirituality is aware of the need for the community of faith continually to examine itself – its ideas, its institutions and its actions – in the light of this revelation, leading to a characteristic pattern of Scripture-nourished recovery, renewal and reform. That pattern first appears definitively at the time of the Reformation itself.

There is much to be learned from the Reformation maxim *ecclesia reformata, ecclesia semper reformanda* – the reformed church must be a church which is always reforming itself. Reformation cannot be seen as a once-for-all event, now firmly located in the past. It must be a present and continuous process. (There is an interesting parallel here with Lenin's notion of a once-for-all revolution, and Trotsky's rival conception of a continuous revolution, always responsive to the needs and opportunities of the moment.) To study the spirituality of the Reformation is thus to be propelled into a new approach to the Christian faith, in which we continually ask what it means to be a Christian, and how this expresses itself at every level – above all, at the interface between faith and life, which we call spirituality.

The Reformation represented an overdue, and hence traumatic, questioning of unquestioned developments in Christian life and thought during the Middle Ages. It posed a challenge to the notion of the irreversibility of history, by suggesting that certain developments in the life and thought of the church during the Middle Ages were improper and illegitimate – and more than that: that they could and should be undone. The Reformation was a quest for Christian authenticity, based on the belief that the medieval church had lost its way and its reason for existence. It represented a willingness to take a profound risk – that of assuming that the foundational resources of the Christian faith could be recovered and applied to the strange world of the sixteenth century, and prove to be vital and relevant. Above all, the Reformation was a quest for Christian roots, grounded in the belief that a community which loses sight of its roots has lost sight of its reason for being in the world in the first place.

In no way does this mean that the reformers saw themselves as attempting to transplant the world of the first-century eastern Mediterranean into the western Europe of the sixteenth. Rather, they believed it was possible and necessary to develop criteria by which the relevance of the foundational events and history of the Christian faith to the present could be established. If Reformation theology and spirituality could be summarised in brief, it is to the effect that past resources possess a vital relevance to the present. By returning to the past, one can become aware of options and possibilities, and catch a glimpse of inspirational visions, which allow one to face the future with new confidence and awareness.

To study the spirituality of the Reformation, then, is not to become preoccupied with some sectarian perspectives. Nor is it to develop an unhealthy interest in a divisive period of Christian history which is inappropriate in our ecumenically minded age (the growing appreciation of Reformation theology and spirituality by Roman Catholic writers is ample evidence of this point). Still less is it to demonstrate an arbitrary antiquarian obsession with a particular period in history, chosen at random. Rather, it is to allow a major formative and creative period in the history of the western Christian church to impinge upon our present-day thinking. The Reformation stands at the dawn of the early modern period, to which we are heirs. At points, its ideas are different from ours. At times, its presuppositions may seem strange. Yet this must not prevent us from engaging in a creative dialogue with the past. A hallmark of theological maturity is a willingness to be challenged by the theological and spiritual legacy of the past. The past must be allowed to question our own presuppositions, and above all our natural tendency to suppose that the ideas, practices and values of our own time are somehow better than those of the past. Yet modern spirituality is not superior to that of the Reformation, merely on account of its being more recent. The classic resources of the Christian faith, such as those of the Reformation, have much to offer all Christians. Just because an idea dates from 1990 does not make it better than one which dates from 1540.

It also has special relevance to those in the modern church who regard themselves as Evangelicals. Protestantism is firmly established as a major and expanding religious force in the modern world. It has, however, become ill-defined. It is no longer clear what it means to be 'Protestant'. What is 'Protestantism'? How may it regain its sense of identity and purpose? What is its fundamental reason for being there? What insights into the gospel, lacking within other Christian traditions, does it possess which justify its continuing existence? Anyone who regards himself or herself as standing within the Protestant tradition needs to rediscover what it means to be *Protestant*.

It also helps to ask if any lessons were learned along the way that might be of use in the future. One of the greatest tragedies that has beset Protestant churches in the present century is a loss of corporate, long-term memory, in favour of a time-scale that spans at best a generation. When you're trying to get somewhere, it helps to know where you've come from. Hindsight leads to foresight, as an enhanced awareness of possibilities dawns. There is a need to recover and value the hard-won insights of earlier generations, and incorporate them into our thinking.

The Reformation marks the origins of a tradition, a way of Christian thinking and acting, which continues to flourish and expand today. It is very easy for a movement such as Protestantism to lose sight of the reasons why it is there. Later Protestantism was witness to a series of developments which often compromised the freshness, vitality and biblical realism of the early Reformation. To many historians of Christian thought, Protestant orthodoxy frequently seems arid and lifeless in comparison with the writings of such seminal thinkers as Luther or Calvin. To return to the Reformation is to recapture that sense of Evangelical simplicity, creativity, freshness and vivacity which later orthodoxy often seems unwittingly to have forfeited. The Reformation possesses a remarkable ability to surprise and delight those who have been brought up within the framework of later forms of Protestantism, gently challenging them to reconsider and reinvigorate their thinking. Karl Barth and Jürgen Moltmann are obvious examples of two modern writers within the Protestant tradition who have been deeply and positively influenced by the ideas of the first glorious days of Protestantism.

To study Reformation spirituality is thus to encounter the foundational ideas of the Protestant tradition. It is to look to the rock from which Evangelicalism was hewn. It is to regain a sense of Evangelical identity and purpose. It is to find an historical reference point from which the problems and opportunities of today may be viewed. There is abundant evidence in recent years that there is a growing desire within Protestant churches worldwide to return to their Evangelical inheritance, mediated to them by the Reformation.

Any theology or spirituality which luxuriates in the habit of ignoring the sources of its vitality runs the risk of becoming rootless and moribund, in that it is unresponsive to and thus uninformed by the sources and resources which give it its distinctive life and being. To study Reformation spirituality and theology is to stand in a responsible relationship to the religious tradition which undergirds Protestantism. It is to re-examine what it is and means to be a Protestant, with a view to reclaiming that distinctiveness and making it available to modern culture.

But what forms of spirituality are associated with the Reformation? The following chapter aims to sketch the outlines of the basic features of this classic form of Evangelical spirituality.

2   The Basic Principles of Reformation Spirituality

The Reformation represents a classic statement of Evangelical spirituality, which is increasingly being recognised as a living option for modern Christianity. It is a resource that *works* – even if it is also a resource that has been neglected. Any attempt to explore the enormous potential of the spirituality of the Reformation for our own day and age must begin with an investigation of its basic features. In what follows, we shall attempt to give a brief yet reliable overview of the basic features of the approaches to spirituality forged at the time of the Reformation. It is helpful to approach the subject from two different angles: first, by considering the forms of spirituality which the reformers regarded as unacceptable; and second, by establishing the basic features of the forms of spirituality which the reformers sought to put in their place. Before turning to this, however, we may consider the term 'spirituality' in a little more detail.

The Nature of Spirituality

In its basic sense, 'spirituality' designates the Christian life – not specifically its *ideas*, but rather the way in which those ideas make themselves visible in the life of Christian individuals and communities. Spirituality represents the interface between ideas and life, between Christian theology and human existence. For the reformers, spirituality concerned the personal and corporate response of believers to the gracious and personal activity of God, embracing virtually every aspect of life. And, as will become clear throughout this work, the spirituality of the Reformation was organically related to its theology. Time and time again, spirituality is seen as the concrete and actual expression of Christian theology, flowing from and nourished by deep theological springs. It would be utterly pointless to reduce Reformation spirituality to a mere catalogue of things we are recommended to do; it is the theological foundations of this spirituality which allow us to value and apply it in our own day and age.

Yet the very phrase 'Reformation spirituality' raises difficulties for some. Many people within the Protestant tradition feel hesitant over using the term 'spirituality', on account of its historical associations with more specifically Catholic forms of the religious life. Words, however, change their meanings over time. The word 'spirituality', shorn of its specifically Catholic associations, has been increasingly adopted within the Protestant tradition. It has progressively come to replace the classical vocabulary of the Protestant tradition, deriving from the Reformation itself. Words such as 'devotion', 'godliness', 'holiness' and 'piety', each with a distinguished history of meaning and usage in its own right, have gradually dropped out of use.

In part, the replacement of these classical terms of the Protestant spiritual tradition with 'spirituality' reflects the increasingly warm relations between Protestants and Roman Catholics, evident at every level of Christian life. Many Protestants no longer feel embarrassed at using a term originally deriving from Catholic writers to describe their interior spiritual search for meaning and wholeness, whether at the individual or communal level, in much the same way as many Roman Catholics no longer feel in the least troubled by drawing on the richness of the resources of the Protestant spiritual tradition. The Christian search for God-given and God-authorised means for the nurture of faith has been pursued vigorously throughout history. The Reformation is no exception to this rule, although its new emphasis upon the need to relate faith and existence in the world added a new dimension to prevailing – and largely monastic – notions of the spiritual life.

Nevertheless, an anxiety must be expressed concerning the use of the term 'spirituality'. It relates to the theological presuppositions, rather than the historical associations, of the term. For the very word 'spirituality' appears to suggest a radical division between the spiritual and the physical, between the soul and the body, between contemplation and everyday life. It implies that its subject is primarily the interior nurture of the soul, undertaken in withdrawal from the distractions of ordinary life. The older vocabulary of the Protestant tradition reflects more faithfully a central aspect of its spirituality – the total integration of faith and everyday life.

This difficulty is largely alleviated if we reclaim the Pauline idea, so faithfully echoed by Luther, of the 'spiritual' as *life in the world orientated towards God*, rather than its classical association of life undertaken in withdrawal from the world. In its fundamental sense, spirituality is concerned with the shaping, empowering and maturing of the 'spiritual person' (*pneumatikos anthropos*), which Paul commends as the fundamental impulse of the life of faith (1 Corinthians 2:14–15) – that is, the person who is alive to and responsive to God in the world, as opposed to the person who merely exists within and responds to the world. There is no difficulty in reclaiming this authentic sense of the term within the Evangelical tradition, with its vital concern – shaped and nourished both by Scripture and the reformers – to map out the contours of responsible Christian living in the world.

A difficulty may be noted before proceeding further. The appeal to 'Reformation spirituality' might be thought to imply that there is a very well defined and narrow outlook on life associated with the Reformation. In fact, the Reformation was a remarkably diverse movement, reflecting the different cultural, social and political situations within which it took place, and differences in education and personality amongst the reformers (to note but a few factors). In my study *The Intellectual Origins of the European Reformation* (1987), I stressed the degree of diversity which could be detected within the Reformation over certain issues of theological method. For example, Luther tends to regard Scripture primarily as relating the promises of God, where Zwingli's stress tends to fall upon the demands for obedience which it contains. At certain points, this leads to major theological differences within the Reformation, reaching a climax in the dispute between Luther and Zwingli over the eucharist. In writing this work, I have tried to make these differing options and approaches available to the reader. However, despite such occasional divergences of method and substance, there is generally sufficient coherence and convergence within the Reformation to justify my use of the phrase 'Reformation spirituality', and to permit me to generalise concerning the outlook of the movement over a number of major issues.

The Criticism of Inauthentic Forms of Spirituality

If the Reformation was concerned with the promotion of Christian spirituality, it was also concerned with the criticism of what it regarded as unacceptable approaches to the matter. Two such approaches were identified as lacking the hallmarks of authentic Christianity. The first relates to the status, the second to the function, of the spiritual director. We shall consider these individually.

The idea of spiritual direction, especially as it centred on the person of the spiritual director, was regarded with considerable suspicion by the reformers, who understood it to be closely linked with such questionable practices and ideas as priestly authority, the monastic life, and indulgences. Within the medieval Catholic tradition, a spiritual director was generally seen as a priest who stood in a position of authority over those whom he directed. Luther's doctrine of the priesthood of all believers served as the foundation for his criticism of these concepts of priesthood. Every Christian was a priest on account of his or her baptism. There was no fundamental difference in status between the ministers of the gospel, by whatever name they might choose to be known, and the ordinary believer.

Medieval Catholicism recognised a fundamental distinction between the 'spiritual estate' (that is, the clergy, whether they were priests, bishops or popes) and the 'temporal estate' (that is, everyone else). Luther declared this distinction to be null and void, a human invention rather than an ordinance of God, in the *Appeal to the German Nobility* (1520):

> All Christians are truly of the spiritual estate, and there is no difference among them except that of function (*Amt*). Paul says in 1 Corinthians 12:12–13 that we are all one body, with every member having its own function by which it serves the others. This is because we have one baptism, one gospel and one faith, and are all Christians, just the same as each other; for baptism, gospel and faith alone make us spiritual and a Christian people . . . And so it follows that there is no true fundamental difference between lay persons and priests, between princes and bishops, between those living in monasteries and those living in the world. The only difference has nothing to do with status, but with the function and work which they perform.

There was no place in Christianity for any notion of a professional class within the church which is in a closer spiritual relationship to God than their fellows.

Nevertheless, not everyone could be allowed to *act* as a priest. As Calvin put this point, 'no Christian in his or her right mind makes everyone equal in the administration of the word and sacraments, in that all things ought to be done decently and in order, and, by the special grace of Christ, ministers are ordained for that purpose.' Just as Luther's doctrine of the priesthood of all believers did not entail the abolition of a professional ministry, neither did it necessarily imply the rejection of spiritual direction. Luther's fundamental principle is that all Christians share the same priestly status (*Stand*) on account of their baptism; they may, however, exercise different functions (*Amt*) within the community of faith, reflecting their individual God-given gifts and abilities. To be a minister is to stand alongside one's fellow-Christians, sharing their status before God; nevertheless, those fellow-believers have recognised the gifts of that individual, and invited him or her, directly or indirectly, to exercise that ministerial function amongst them. The recognition of the *equality* of all believers must not be understood to imply the *identity* of all believers.

In his treatise *Concerning the Ministry* (1523), Luther argued that all believers share in the priesthood of Christ as High Priest, on account of being united to him through faith. But this does not, he insisted, imply that all believers are *called* to be priests. He suggested that the selection of ministers should take place in the following way. Members of the church should meet together and pray for the guidance of the Holy Spirit upon them individually and as a community. Having done this, they should make their choice of minister. This person is then presented and commended to the community of faith as one who has been called to the office and work of a minister of the gospel. This did not amount to a permanent change in the status of the person thus selected; the community could subsequently choose additional or alternative persons to act in this way. All Christians are given the status of priests; the exercise of that function is nevertheless conditional upon the approval of the people of God.

So it is with spiritual direction, which remains a real and important option within the Reformation tradition. In no way did the Reformation witness the abolition of spiritual direction; rather, it saw this process being placed in its proper context. The idea of a spiritual director being an individual with some exclusive knowledge of God, or with some superior status within the church, or some exclusive relationship to God which set him apart from his fellow-believers, is vigorously rejected. The spiritual director, like the minister, is one who stands alongside the people of God, sharing their situation and status. Nevertheless, the community of faith, or individuals within that community, recognises that God has given some of its members special gifts, such as the gift of spiritual discernment and wisdom, and chooses to allow these gifts to be exercised in its midst. The spiritual director is thus seen as a spiritual friend, a colleague rather than a superior.

In many ways, Luther's approach may be seen as recapturing the lost ideals of monastic spirituality. The monastic movement had its origins partly in a flight from an understanding of the Christian life which rigorously excluded the laity from any spiritual authority within the church. The monk was originally one who chose to by-pass the increasingly centralised hierarchy of the institutional church, in order to recover the apostolic idea of the vocation of the ordinary Christian. The monastic movement of the fourth and fifth centuries was primarily a protest against the marginalisation of the laity in matters of spirituality and spiritual authority. By his very existence, the monk was a silent protest against the growing priestly authoritarianism of the early church. Anthony of Egypt, perhaps the most famous of such monks, remained a layman.

At Nitria, the great monastic community south-east of Alexandria in the Nile delta, there were a mere eight priests amongst the community of five thousand monks in the fourth century. The remainder were laymen – probably rather anti-clerical laymen – convinced that the spiritual lives and needs of individual lay people were being overlooked amidst the new organisational developments of the church. Where Cyprian of Carthage tended to think of the church as a quasi-imperial institution, spiritually governed by bishops, priests and deacons, the early monastic movement kept alive the foundational insight of the vocation of the ordinary believer. If this insight was lost during the Middle Ages, it was due in no small part to the increasingly routine ordination of monks. The Reformation recovery of the 'call of the laity', given theological expression in the doctrine of the priesthood of all believers and firmly embedded in the structures of Reformation spirituality, may be seen as picking up this central feature of early monastic spirituality, in order to recapture the power of its vision in early modern Europe.

The second unacceptable approach centred upon an understanding of the function of the spiritual director. In his major reforming work of 1520, *The Babylonian Captivity of the Christian Church*, Luther protested vigorously against what he regarded as a false understanding of the nature of the function of the priest. Take baptism, he suggested. The place, power and purpose of baptism are not dependent upon the person of the priest, but upon the promises of God. It is not the priest who achieves anything; it is God. The function of the priest is to allow God to work in and through him, not to achieve anything in his own right. Something is done through, not done by, the priest. (Luther, incidentally, is also protesting against the popular medieval view that sacraments gained their efficacy through the personal qualities and achievements of those who enacted them.)

A similar misunderstanding attached itself to spiritual direction in the late Middle Ages. On the eve of the Reformation, the spiritual director was viewed as one who achieved something for those whom he directed. Spiritual growth was often seen as something the spiritual director himself brought about. Such was the emphasis placed upon the person of the director, that the efficacy of spiritual direction was often held to be dependent upon the personal qualities and merits of the director. The reformers were understandably anxious over such approaches, which played down the role of God in spiritual growth, and led to something of a personality cult among spiritual directors. Spiritual direction was to be undertaken by those willing to understand that their function was that of being open to God. In spiritual growth, it is God, not the spiritual director, who brings about maturity of faith.

Once more, this insight sets spiritual direction in its proper perspective; it does not demand its elimination. Indeed, late medieval spirituality was far from lacking any awareness of the importance and priority of God in relation to spiritual growth. The reformers may be regarded as reclaiming an authentic element of Christian spirituality, which had become obscured or neglected through the increasing trend towards professionalisation within spiritual direction, with a resulting loss of a sense of vocation – of being *called* to be a spiritual director.

The basic point at issue has, in any case, been well taken since the time of the Reformation. Although there will always be those who see the process as that of a master shaping his pupils after his own likeness, responsible Christian spiritual direction rests upon an awareness on the part of both the director and the directed of the need to be open and responsive to God. It is God, not the director, who brings about growth and maturity. Tilden Edwards makes the point as follows in his work *Spiritual Friend*:

Being a spiritual friend is being the physician of a wounded soul. And what does a physician do when someone comes with a bleeding wound? Three things. He or she cleanses the wound, aligns the parts, and gives it rest. That's all. The physician does *not* heal. He or she provides an *environment* for the dominant natural process of healing to take its course. The physician is really a midwife rather than a healer.

The spiritual director thus aims to provide an environment for the nourishment of faith, in the full knowledge that it is God who creates, nourishes and sustains faith. This vital perspective, central to Reformation spirituality, is now the common coinage of responsible Christian spiritual direction.

The Reformation thus cleared the ground for responsible approaches to spirituality. The inauthentic and irresponsible views of some late medieval spiritual writers were set to one side; the way was made clear for the reclamation and reappropriation of the authentic spirituality of the period, the voice of which had been stifled on the eve of the Reformation. As we shall see, however, the Reformation did not merely involve reclaiming old ideas; it involved the forging of new approaches to spirituality, suited to the demands and opportunities of the new age which we now call the early modern period. We can illustrate this point by considering the place of the theologian in Reformation thought.

In the Middle Ages, theologians were often equally isolated from the community of faith. They were generally individuals, like the great Thomas Aquinas, who were based in the majestic monasteries of Europe. They were closeted within the confines of the monastic life, and wrote – when they wrote at all – for an audience of their fellow monks. It is rare – but happily, as the example of Thomas à Kempis reminds us, not totally unknown – to find a medieval theologian operating outside this context.

In our own day and age, theologians have become increasingly detached from the communities which they are meant to serve. They have become more and more professionalised, isolated within academic theological faculties, and vulnerable to the charge of dwelling within ivory towers. Professionalisation has tended to remove theologians from within the communities of faith, and placed them within the narrow confines of the universities. Secularisation has led to a separation of personal faith and academic life; the professional academic theologian need not have any commitment to the faith or life of the church.

The Reformation bridges the gap between these two unsatisfactory approaches to the function of theology. The reformers, however diverse their origins may have been, were individuals who were based in the cities of Europe, living within the communities which they served, and sharing their faith. They were isolated by neither monastery nor university from the people who looked to them for guidance. Their task was to interpret and apply the gospel to the concrete situations in which they found themselves – above all, in relating to the lives of ordinary people.

Perhaps one of the most important moments of the Reformation may be traced to 1520, when Luther made the crucial and dramatic decision to cease being a purely academic reformer, addressing academic issues and audiences, and instead to make a direct and passionate appeal to the religious hopes and faith of the German people. Luther became both a preacher and a pastor – and his pastoral concern and experience shows up, time and time again, in his theology. Luther read and interpreted the New Testament as one who believed that this document was of vital and continuing relevance to the life of the Christian community (another stark contrast between the theologians of the Reformation period and the manner in which the New Testament is handled in much modern academia). Here is a genuine pastoral theology, a theology which addresses the needs and concerns of ordinary believers, and those who seek to minister to them.

Similarly, throughout Calvin's writings, we find a determination to engage with the real world of everyday life in the city of Geneva, along with all the problems and possibilities this brings with it. It seems that Calvin learned the lessons which Reinhold Niebuhr learned in downtown Detroit during the 1920s. In his *Leaves from the Notebook of a Tamed Cynic* (1929), Niebuhr wrote:

> If a minister wants to be a man among men he need only stop creating a devotion to abstract ideals which everyone accepts in

theory and denies in practice, and to agonize about their validity and practicability in the social issues which he and others face in our present civilization. That immediately gives his ministry a touch of reality and potency.

Precisely this pattern stands out in Calvin's spiritual and homiletic writings. Calvin addresses real and specific human situations – social, political and economic – with all the risks that this precision entails. Here is no abstract theorising, conducted in the refined atmosphere of an ivory tower. Rather, here is a theologian sharing the life of his people, and attempting to interpret and apply the gospel in that situation. Calvin wrote, worshipped and preached as a member of the community which he addressed. He was not apart from them; he was not above them; rather, he wrote from within his community, as part of it, sharing its life and its problems. Here is no theology imposed from above or from outside, but a theology generated within a community, with the needs, possibilities and aspirations of that community in mind.

Is there not a model here which has relevance and appeal for today? Again and again, ordinary Christians today comment on how irrelevant they consider theologians to be. 'They seem so distant.' 'They don't seem to understand the problems of everyday life.' 'They seem to have a totally different agenda from ordinary believers.' 'We can't understand what they are going on about.' While working in the United States, I even heard the following criticism of certain theologians teaching at major North American seminaries: 'These guys don't even go to church – why should we listen to them?' 'There is no way that these people present us with role models suitable for Christian ministry.'

In brief, academic theology gets a very bad popular press. These comments are deeply revealing, indicating the considerable gulf that has opened up between the academy and the church. Surely, many ask, there must be a more satisfactory way of conceiving the task, calling and responsibilities of the theologian? It is thus vitally important to note that the Reformation offers a very different model, with a distinguished history of

application within the Christian tradition. The theologian oper-
ates within the community, addressing its needs and concerns.
(There are strong echoes and endorsements here of the Eastern
Orthodox idea of the theologian as one who prays properly.) In
short: the theologian is one who is called to serve the community
of faith from within. Part of that service is criticism of its ideas
and outlooks – but it is a loving and caring criticism on the
basis of shared Christian beliefs and commitments, rather than
the modern criticism of the Christian community by academic
'theologians' on the basis of secular beliefs and values, often
radically agnostic or atheistic, which that community feels no
pressing reason to share. Criticism of a community is a sign
and a consequence of commitment to that community.

To study the spirituality of the Reformation, then, is to
become aware of different ways of doing things, different
ways of approaching problems, different ways of presenting
and contextualising the Christian proclamation, which can act
as a stimulus and catalyst to us in the modern period. Business
corporations have long appreciated the value of idea-generating
sessions, in which ideas and options are pooled, prior to being
evaluated. Think of Reformation spirituality as contributing ideas
to that pool. It is a resource at our disposal. This naturally
leads us to consider the basic features of this spirituality in
more detail.

Distinguishing Features of Reformation Spirituality

Four basic themes can be discerned as underlying the spirituality
of the Reformation.

1. It is grounded and nourished in the study of Scripture. The
sola scriptura principle, so central to the theological method of
the reformers, is equally evident in their spirituality. Scripture
is the supreme God-authorised and God-given resource for the
generation and nourishment of Christian faith. The history of the
leading personalities of the Reformation indicates the centrality
of the reading of and meditation upon Scripture. Marguerite of

Navarre, one of the leading French Evangelicals of the early sixteenth century, came to a new understanding and experience of her faith as a result of such a process. As a result, she was pilloried by students at the University of Paris. On 1 October 1533, a student comedy portrayed her as a housewife who became mentally deranged after reading her Bible. (Incidentally, we have an account of this episode from the pen of Calvin himself.) Mockery seemed to be just about the only way of coping with this deeply threatening development.

The centrality of Scripture for Reformation spirituality can be seen from the literary resources made available by the reformers. Three are of especial importance.

i) The *biblical commentary* aimed to allow its readers to peruse and understand the word of God, explaining difficult phrases, identifying points of importance, and generally allowing its readers to become familiar with the thrust and concerns of the biblical passage. Writers such as Calvin, Luther, Melanchthon and Zwingli produced commentaries aimed at a variety of readerships, both academic and lay.

ii) The *expository sermon* aimed to fuse the horizons of the scriptural texts and its hearers, applying the principles underlying the scriptural passage to the situation of the audience. Calvin's sermons at Geneva are a model of their kind. It was Calvin who developed the notion of *lectio continua* – the continuous preaching through a scriptural book, rather than on passages drawn from a lectionary or chosen by the preacher. For example, during the period between 20 March 1555 to 15 July 1556, Calvin is known to have preached some two hundred sermons on a single scriptural book – Deuteronomy.

iii) Works of *biblical theology*, such as Calvin's *Institutes of the Christian Religion*, aimed to allow their readers to gain an appreciation of the theological coherence of Scripture, by bringing together and synthesising its statements on matters of theological importance. By this means, readers of Scripture were enabled to establish a coherent and consistent world-view, which would undergird their everyday lives. The French historian Pierre Imbart de La Tour once wrote: 'The first work of Calvin was a book – the *Institutes*. The second was a city –

Geneva. Book and city complement one another. One is doctrine formulated; the other is doctrine applied.' For Calvin, as for the reformers in general, Scripture moulded doctrine, which in turn shaped the realities of Christian life. Reformation spirituality is thus, in the first place, scriptural, and in the second, doctrinal.

Through these three main literary resources, the reformers sought to inculcate within their readers a Scripture-centred and Scripture-based outlook on life. These resources were, however, seen as ancillary works, which aimed to supplement Scripture, rather than replace it. As Calvin remarked, 'We speak where Scripture speaks, and are silent where Scripture is silent'. The fundamental assumption underlying them all is that their readers will have access to the scriptural text, and that they merely need help in interpreting and applying it.

It may be noted at this point that the 'Scripture principle' has been seriously misunderstood, both by those sympathetic to the Reformation tradition, and by those critical of it. Two particular misunderstandings need to be identified and addressed. In the first place, the Reformation emphasis upon the priority of Scripture was not understood to place the opinions of the individual above the corporate judgement of the church. In the second, it did not entail the marginalisation of other spiritual and theological resources. We may consider both these points, and their relevance for Reformation spirituality, individually.

Many writers of the radical wing of the Reformation – often still referred to as 'Anabaptism' – held that every individual had the right to interpret Scripture in whatever way he or she pleased. This right was viewed almost as a fundamental Christian liberty, reflecting the egalitarianism (economic, political and religious) so characteristic of this movement. The mainstream of the Reformation, however, adopted a significantly different approach to the relation between the individual and communal interpretations of Scripture. Recognising that the church theoretically could misunderstand Scripture at points – and that, as a matter of history, it had in fact done so – the reformers held that individuals had the right to challenge the church over points of interpretation. The received doctrinal and spiritual tradition of the church had to be constantly checked out against Scripture, to ensure that it was faithful to what it purported to represent. Luther argued that the medieval church's teaching on justification by faith was way out of line with the New Testament, and that this teaching would thus have to be re-aligned with its scriptural foundation. Zwingli developed similar points in relation to the theology of the sacraments, and Calvin in relation to the theology of the church.

But the reformers had no intention of beginning *de novo*. They did not see themselves as starting doctrinal and spiritual reflection all over again, or as constructing a *new* doctrinal and spiritual tradition. Rather, they saw themselves as critically evaluating the existing traditions, with a view to reforming and renewing them, where this was necessary in the light of their scriptural foundations. Increasingly, scholars have pointed out how medieval theology did not regard tradition as a source of revelation independent of Scripture; rather, it was a particular way of reading Scripture. Tradition is primarily a *traditional manner of reading and interpreting Scripture*. The reformers were concerned to ensure that this traditional way of reading Scripture was actually faithful to Scripture itself.

In the second place, it should be noted that the reformers' emphasis upon the total priority of Scripture as a theological resource did not prevent them from reading and valuing the theological writings of the Christian tradition. Scripture constituted the centre of gravity of their thought – yet it did not define the boundaries of their reading. Other writings were received and valued, where they were seen to be consistent with Scripture. Thus both Luther and Calvin frequently placed on record their admiration for the writings of Augustine, and made this tangible by frequently referring to him, and making liberal use of his ideas, in their writings. On the other hand, Luther had little patience with much to be found in the writings of the fifteenth-century writer Gabriel Biel, whose ideas he generally regarded as a serious deviation from Scripture. In general, the reformers prized and made good use of theological and spiritual writings, where they were reliable and responsible interpretations of Scripture.

The reformers thus had no quarrel with the traditional doctrinal and spiritual teachings of the church – provided it could be shown that they were in line with Scripture. Two examples – one theoretical, one practical – may be noted to illustrate this point. Although, strictly speaking, the doctrine of the Trinity is not explicitly stated in Scripture, the reformers regarded this component of the doctrinal tradition of the church as being thoroughly consistent with Scripture, and capable of being derived from it. They thus had no hesitation in endorsing this doctrine as scriptural and authentically Christian. Equally, the practice of infant baptism is not explicitly recognised and sanctioned by Scripture. Luther, Calvin and Zwingli, however, argued that it was perfectly consistent with Scripture, and was to be accepted and valued for that reason.

In the specific case of spirituality, the same approach was adopted. The reformers had no difficulty with the Catholic spiritual tradition, provided it was seen to be in line with Scripture. To embrace the ideas and values of the Reformation in no way implies the rejection of the Christian spiritual tradition prior to 1500! Rather, it merely involves a willingness to check out this tradition against its scriptural roots: where it was clearly scriptural, it could be warmly embraced; where it was contradicted by Scripture, it was to be rejected. Thus the reformers were appreciative of many aspects of Benedictine spirituality, not least on account of its emphasis upon the importance of reading and meditation upon Scripture; whereas they were sceptical of certain types of Franciscan spirituality, such as the vow of absolute poverty, which they regarded as not resting upon adequate scriptural foundations.

The contemporary implications of this will be evident. Those who regard themselves as standing within the Reformation tradition are at liberty to draw upon the substantial resources of the Catholic and Orthodox spiritual traditions, provided these are seen to be consistent with Scripture. For example, many Protestants find Ignatian spirituality, especially its use of the religious imagination to reflect upon key Gospel passages, deeply stimulating and conducive to the growth of faith. It does not matter that this technique was developed by one of the leading opponents of the Reformation in the sixteenth century! The important question centres on whether it is consistent with Scripture (which is clearly the case).

In practice, of course, Protestants do modify Ignatian spirituality in a significant manner, tending to eliminate its monastic origins and influences, in order to yield a version of this spirituality capable of being used *in* – instead of apart from – the everyday world. (As we shall see, the reformers were deeply hostile to any notion of withdrawing from the world, seeing the believer's responsibility to be that of remaining within the world.) Here is an excellent example of the positive and creative interaction of the Protestant and Catholic spiritual traditions, without compromising the fundamental principles of the former. Indeed, the new interest in what might loosely be called 'biblical spirituality' within Catholicism (a phenomenon increasingly referred to as 'Catholic Evangelicalism') is likely to be further nourished and sustained by this positive, yet critical, attitude on the part of Evangelicals.

If the Reformation emphasis upon Scripture led to a more responsible and critical attitude to the spiritual authority of tradition, it also led to a more reliable attitude to personal experience. Many of the more radical performers argued that individual experience was a perfectly reliable and authoritative guide to spiritual truth. Scripture could be dispensed with. The idea of personal revelation through the Holy Spirit was treated with scepticism by the mainstream reformers. Experience needs to be interpreted in the light of Scripture. Scripture is an objective and communal resource; private experience is an individual and subjective matter. The mainstream Reformation emphasis upon Scripture liberates the church from the tyranny of self-styled prophets, possessing personal revelations from God, denied to the community of faith as a whole.

Martin Luther once attended a conference at which some representatives of the more radical prophetic and visionary wing of the Reformation were speaking. He heard one of them relate his visions and personal divine revelations at some length. After this lengthy sermon drew to a close, Luther uttered a single sentence – a sentence which both summarised the content and destroyed the credibility of what he had just heard: 'You have mentioned nothing of Scripture'. The mainstream Reformation emphasis upon the sufficiency and authority of Scripture liberates us from the oppression of powerful personalities who declare that God has important things to say, other than what is to be found in Scripture – and who then proceed to insist that *they* are in personal possession of these new insights. No personal word of God to anyone can ever be allowed to have the same authority as Scripture. Scripture possesses authority for a community; a personal vision has purely individual authority, if it has any authority at all.

Much of what passes as modern Evangelicalism, especially in the United States, has completely lost sight of this principle. It has become intoxicated with the egocentrism so characteristic of the secular world. The American televangelist Oral Roberts once held up a Bible in front of his television cameras, and declared: 'There is so much more God has to say than can be found within the covers of this one book.' (He then moved on to indicate what else God had to say to his audience, based on his personal insights and visions.) Robert Schuller, pastor of the Evangelical Crystal Cathedral in Orange County, southern California, argued that while 'the sixteenth-century Reformation returned our focus to the sacred Scriptures as the only infallible rule for faith and practice, the new reformation will return our focus to the sacred right of every person to self-esteem!' This easy-going accommodation to the secular values of southern California has alarming spiritual results: human self-esteem comes to take the place of the self-revelation of God as a criterion of truth. Much of modern Evangelicalism has, quite simply, abandoned – whether deliberately or accidentally – its birthright at this point.

2. Reformation spirituality insists that the quest for human identity, authenticity and fulfilment cannot be undertaken in isolation from God. To find out *who* we are – and *why* we are – is to find out who God is, and what he is like. Calvin states this principle with characteristic lucidity in the opening sentence of the 1559 edition of his *Institutes of the Christian Religion*:

Nearly all the wisdom we possess, that is to say, true and sound wisdom, consists of two parts: the knowledge of God and of ourselves. And although they are closely connected, it is difficult to say which comes first . . . Knowledge of ourselves not only stimulates us to seek God but, as it were, also leads us by the hand to find him . . . We never achieve a clear knowledge of ourselves until we have first looked upon God's face, and then descend from contemplating him to examine ourselves.

Any notion of spirituality as a quest for heightened religious experience as an end in itself is totally alien to the outlook of the Reformation. Equally, any idea that it is possible to have a detached or disinterested knowledge of God is excluded. To know God is to be changed by God.

There is thus a substantial doctrinal foundation to Reformation spirituality. Nevertheless, an interest in doctrine is not necessarily regarded as equivalent to an interest in spirituality. For example, both Luther and Calvin strongly criticised scholastic theology, on account of its tendency on the one hand to drive a wedge between theological reflection and spirituality, between the head and the heart, and on the other its failure to relate to the existential aspects of faith. There can be no cerebralisation of faith. As Calvin stated this point in the 1539 edition of the *Institutes*:

Doctrine is not a matter of the tongue, but of life. It is not apprehended only by the intellect and memory, like other branches of learning, but is received only when it possesses the whole soul . . . We assign priority to doctrine, in which our religion is contained, since by it our salvation begins; but it must be transfused into our hearts, and pass into our conduct, and thus transform us into itself . . . The gospel ought to penetrate the innermost feelings of the heart, fix its seat in the soul, and pervade the entire person a hundred times more than the frigid writings of the philosophers.

Calvin's emphasis upon the experiential aspects of our knowledge of God (a serious embarrassment, incidentally, to those who stolidly persist in portraying him as insensitive to spiritual experience, or woodenly intellectualist or cerebral) reflects the common Reformation belief: to know God is to experience the power of God. To know God is to be changed by God. 'The knowledge of God which we are invited to develop is not the sort that is content with empty speculation, which just rattles around inside our heads, but a knowledge which proves to be substantial and fruitful in our hearts.'

Luther makes a similar point in his *Liberty of a Christian* (1520), stressing the way in which the believer comes to share in, and be transformed by, the promises of God. A range of powerful images jostle for attention as Luther tries to give expression to the dynamic manner in which knowledge of God changes us – we are united to his promises, we are absorbed into them, we are saturated and intoxicated by them.

> Since these promises of God are holy, true, righteous, free, and peaceful words, full of goodness, the soul which clings to them with a firm faith will be so closely united with them and altogether absorbed into them that it will not only share in all their power, but will be saturated and intoxicated by them. If a touch of Christ healed, how much more will this most tender spiritual touch, this absorbing of the Word, communicate to the soul all things which belong to the Word.

Knowledge of God is thus like a vital force, capable of changing those who possess it and are possessed by it. True knowledge of God moves us to worship, obedience and the hope of eternal life. Calvin stresses that there is no knowledge of God where there is no faith and worship of God. It is only in knowing God that we come to know ourselves – although, as Calvin pointed out with equal vigour, it is only by knowing ourselves fully that we come to know God fully. Knowledge of ourselves and knowledge of God are given together – or they are not given at all.

This robust assertion has important consequences, as Calvin points out. In the first place, it further consolidates the centrality of Scripture for Reformation spirituality, as noted above. Reliable and authoritative knowledge of God is only to be had from this source. In the second, however, it points to the importance of Christology. In Jesus Christ, we are presented with the holding together of divinity and humanity, God and man, in a single and indivisible unity. It is here that the characteristically *Christian* knowledge of God and knowledge of human nature converge and come to a point of focus. Christ is 'the mathematical point of Scripture' (Luther). The manner in which many spiritual writings within the Reformation tradition centre upon considering the example of Jesus Christ reflects this basic theological affirmation. 'Christ, through whom we have been restored to favour with God, is set before us as a model' (Calvin).

If these insights are applied to the modern period, it will be evident that the extensive appeal made to secular psychological and psychoanalytical disciplines in much recent spirituality needs to be criticised. Although the notions of 'human fulfilment' found in such secular systems are often profoundly unChristian, and require a critical examination hitherto generally absent on the part of those who appeal to them, my fundamental point here is simply this: psychology is not theology. To draw upon insights concerning the human condition is only half of the story that Christian spirituality is concerned to tell; indeed, if only half of that story is told, it has not been properly and authentically told at all. Knowledge of God and knowledge of ourselves are the essential components of an authentic and responsible spirituality, according to the Reformation tradition. To base a spirituality solely upon the insights of secular psychology or psychotherapy is to forfeit both the use of the term 'Christian', and the insights which the Christian knowledge of God in Christ brings in its wake. Psychology alone cannot, and should not be allowed to, become the fundamental resource of Christian spirituality. If the Reformation has anything to say to the present generation, it is simply this: don't lose sight of God. Pop psychology makes sloppy theology which makes for mushy Christianity. A vigorous dose of real theology gives intellectual backbone and stamina to faith. And faith needs such reinforcement, in the muddled and confused world of the late twentieth century.

3. Reformation spirituality explicitly recognises the priesthood and vocation of all Christian believers. It is here that a decisive

and irrevocable accommodation to the realities of the new social situation of early modern Europe may be seen. And yet in making this accommodation to the new social realities, the reformers believed that they were in no way compromising the essence of Christianity. Instead, they were reclaiming the notion of the laity as the people (*laos*) of God. Spirituality is a resource to be placed at the disposal of the entire church, rather than a specific section of its membership (such as its clergy). In practical terms, this expresses itself chiefly in the obvious tendency for writers within the Reformation tradition to address themselves primarily to a lay audience. While acknowledging the practical importance of clergy and other church leaders in developing the spiritual depth of their communities, followers of the Reformation tradition located this role in their function as educators, rather than their status as persons. In principle and in practice, the Reformation tradition expects to find and value spiritual direction among its laity.

Central to Reformation spirituality is the recovery of the notion of the laity as the *laos* – the people of God. The publication of Erasmus of Rotterdam's *Handbook of the Christian Soldier* (1503) may be said to have undermined the credibility of any conception of the Christian life which placed the clergy permanently upon a totally different level – whether ontological or functional, whether theoretical or practical – from the remainder of believers. For Erasmus, the clergy had but one function: to enable the laity to achieve the same degree of knowledge and understanding of the resources of the Christian faith as they themselves possessed. They were educators, charged with the task of eliminating the educational gap between themselves and the laity.

In the early Middle Ages, learning was virtually the exclusive preserve of the clergy. Yet as the European Renaissance made literacy and education widely available, the divide of learning between the clergy and the laity became radically diminished. For Erasmus, religion was an inner spiritual affair, in which the individual believer seeks to deepen his or her knowledge of God by the reading of Scripture. The educated laity thus came to achieve a degree of understanding of their faith hitherto unrealised. Increasingly, they gained confidence in their ability to read Scripture for themselves, and to develop a lay piety. As the newly emerging professional classes began to gain power in the cities, gradually wresting control from the old patrician families, they brought to their practice and interpretation of the Christian faith much the same critical acumen and professionalism that they employed in their secular careers. This development opened the way for an increasingly critical lay assessment of the abilities of the clergy, and growing lay confidence in religious matters.

Of importance here is the new confidence evident among women to understand and interpret the Christian faith for themselves, which became especially evident within the noble families of France, Italy, Germany and England. The new emphasis upon the laity was regarded with horror by many at the time. Cardinal Cajetan, charged with handling the Lutheran crisis in Germany, believed that the inevitable (and shocking) outcome of the new reforming movements was that women would become accepted as theologians. The French reformer Étienne Le Court was burned alive at Rouen in Normandy for teaching that women would proclaim the gospel. Jacques Lefèvre d'Étaples pointedly dedicated his French translation of the New Testament 'to all Christian men *and women*'; he had no doubts that its readership would – and should – include this hitherto marginalised component of the people of God. In his *Women of the Reformation*, Roland Bainton has given us a fine account of aspects of this important development, viewed through the prism of the lives of leading women of the sixteenth century. In practice, the Reformation tended to adopt socially conservative approaches to the role of women, perhaps on account of a reluctant social realism: society was perhaps not yet ready for this radical new social development, even if its theological basis had been securely and irreversibly established.

It is to this educated lay readership, male and female, that the spirituality of the Reformation made its appeal in the early modern period. Its audience was lay, not clerical; the resources upon which it drew were biblical, rather than the textbooks of scholastic theology or ecclesiastical theory. This development can be seen by considering the contents of lay libraries of the period. Most upper-class families in fifteenth-century Florence owned personal copies of the New Testament. An examination of the personal libraries of sixteenth-century French middle class families also reveals how the resources for a biblically based spirituality were widely available at the time of the Reformation. Lefèvre's French New Testament of 1523 and his French Psalter of 1524, were widely read throughout France, and were even distributed free of charge within the evangelically minded diocese of Meaux. Copies of these works, along with the New Testament commentaries of Erasmus, Melanchthon and Lefèvre himself, were frequently to be found jostling for space on the bookshelves of French households. Commentaries upon Scripture, especially the New Testament, soon became one of the most important resources for personal private theological and spiritual study. Bullinger, Luther, Melanchthon and Zwingli are but four of those who made available such vital resources to meet the needs of a biblically orientated laity. It is, however, widely agreed that the most important work to appeal to this readership was a commentary not so much on a specific scriptural writing, as upon the entirety of the contents of Scripture.

Calvin's *Institutes of the Christian Religion*, easily one of the most important books of the sixteenth century, is conceived primarily as a guide to the theological and spiritual richness of Scripture as a whole. Calvin declared that his purpose in writing this work was to allow his readers to have easy access to the Word of God, and to progress in it without stumbling. The enormous success of this work, which was reprinted, both in full and in various abridged forms, in numerous vernacular translations, bears witness to the importance of its envisaged audience – a literate laity, with a genuine thirst to wrestle with the full resources of the Christian faith.

That same readership is very much in evidence today. Daily Bible notes and biblical commentaries, both devotional and more scholarly in character, find a substantial market amongst those ordinary believers who regard Scripture as the origin and foundation of their faith. Small groups, usually entirely lay, meet regularly for Bible study. Time and time again, as the literature devoted to church growth regularly informs us, such groups function as centres of expansion and development. It is no accident that Protestantism was spread, both spontaneously and by deliberate organisation, in sixteenth-century France by precisely such groups. The *églises plantées*, the powerhouses of Calvin's attempts to evangelise his native France, were first and foremost small groups of laity who met regularly for prayer and the study of Scripture. A similar need, a similar audience, and a similar possibility for growth and consolidation exist today. The spirituality of the Reformation is directed to precisely such an audience. Will it have the same effect today? The Christian world of today is the laboratory in which this possibility can be tested.

4. Reformation spirituality is grounded in and orientated towards life in the everyday world, enabling Christians to involve themselves firmly and fully in the life of the secular order, while at the same time lending it new meaning and depth. Once more, a decisive accommodation to the social realities of the early modern period may be discerned – yet without any compromise in relation to the essence of the gospel. The monastic notion of 'the contempt of the world' (Thomas à Kempis) is decisively rejected, at least in regard to its consequences for life in the everyday world.

The primary focus of the reformers' positive attitudes towards the world centred upon the great institutions of state and society. It was here that Christian faith was to be put into action. There is, however, a sense in which the home replaced the monastery as the arena within which Christian spirituality was to be applied and focused. The extended household was a society in miniature, within which the Christian faith was to be lived out. The home, like society as a whole, was an area in which faith could be put into practice. The key elements of Reformation spirituality – most notably, the doctrine of justification by faith and the work ethic – brought new levels of meaning and significance to even the most routine of domestic duties. George Herbert captures this aspect of Reformation spirituality perfectly with his lines:

> A servant with this clause
> Makes drudgery divine.
> Who sweeps a room, as for thy laws,
> Makes that and the action fine.

The Reformation propensity for lending new vitality to mundane existence soon demonstrated itself to have considerable potential for the emerging professional classes of early modern Europe. The modern west is heir to this development, and can be heir to the spiritual resources which undergirded this world- and work-affirming outlook. The integration of Christian life and theology gave a new importance both to commitment to and investment in the world, and to the study of the resources of the Christian faith. These two activities, which can too easily go their separate ways, are welded together in an inner unity by the dynamics of Reformation spirituality, a theme which will be explored further in chapters 6 and 7 of this work.

Above all, the Reformation recalls us to commitment to and action within the everyday world. Just as the reformers rejected a retreat to the monasteries, so their modern heirs must reject a retreat into the narrow withdrawn confines of Christian subculture. The world at its worst needs Christians at their best – and studying the spirituality of the Reformation puts resources that have been tried and tested in some of the toughest tracks of life into the hands of believers. Christians are meant to live and work in the world, just as they are meant to be nourished and encouraged in their faith within the church. The church nourishes believers, in order that they may go out into the world to glorify, serve and proclaim God. To withdraw from the world is to deny God the chance to work through you in the world. You cannot be the salt of the world or the light of the world if you never venture *into* the world! As we shall see, the Reformation developed sophisticated and reliable ways of allowing Christians to become deeply involved in the affairs of the world, while maintaining both their Christian integrity, and their Christian faith.

Having sketched the principles which undergird the spirituality of the Reformation, we may now begin to explore it in more detail. The reformers did not invent a new religion: they purified and renewed a religion that was already there. And how was this to be done? By returning to the roots of faith, in order to be refreshed, nourished and challenged – a theme which we shall explore in the next chapter.

3   Rediscovering Christian Roots: Spirituality and Identity

Recognition of the need to recover a sense of Christian identity and purpose pervades the writings of the reformers. There was a feeling that Christianity needed to be reborn and reshaped. It was not merely that medieval forms of Christianity were of limited relevance to the new era of human history then dawning; it was that those medieval forms of Christianity represented distortions of authentic Christianity. Time and time again, the writings of the reformers develop the following theme: there is an urgent need to return to the roots of faith, and reappropriate an authentic form of the Christian gospel. Authenticity is the touchstone of relevance: an authentic gospel will be a relevant and a stable gospel.

The idea of returning to one's roots is as complex as it is powerful, and needs careful examination before its full potential can be appreciated. We can begin to catch a sense of its relevance by considering the importance of this theme for the Italian Renaissance – that great period in European history when, in the words of Paolo Giovio, culture was 'born again'.

A Case Study: The Cultural Roots of the Italian Renaissance

The Italian Renaissance is rightly regarded as one of the most important and creative periods in European culture. The art galleries and museums of the world are packed full of exhibits showing the remarkable originality and imagination of the new culture which took hold of northern Italy during the period 1350–1550. By the end of the sixteenth century, virtually all of western Europe had been infected by this astonishing enthusiasm and vision. But what lay behind this magnificent outburst of energy, of incredible artistic excitement, at the time?

The answer to this question is complex. However, a substantial part of that answer can be stated in two Latin words – *ad fontes*, 'back to the original sources'. Italian culture gained a new sense of purpose and dignity by seeing itself as the modern heir and champion of the long-dead culture of classical Rome. The Italian Renaissance could be said to be about bringing the culture of ancient Rome back to life in the modern period. The imaginations of artists, architects, poets, writers and theologians were seized by this vision. Imagine being able to allow the glory of the past to interact with the cultural void of fourteenth-century Italy! And as the process of recollection began, Italy began to gain a reputation as the cradle of a new civilisation in Europe.

It is no accident that Italy was the birthplace and cradle of the Renaissance. The Italian writers of the period appear to have seen themselves as returning to their cultural roots, in the world of classical Rome. A stream, they argued, was purest at its source; why not return to that source, instead of being satisfied with the muddy and stagnant waters of existing contemporary culture? The past was seen as a resource, a foundational influence, whose greatness demanded that it should be allowed a voice in the present. The Italian Renaissance arose through a decision to allow the historic roots of Italian culture to impose upon the present, to inform it, to stimulate it – and to transform it. The explosion of creativity which resulted is an eloquent and powerful witness to the potential effects of returning to cultural roots, and allowing them to impact upon the present. The excitement of the Renaissance rediscovery of the past was tempered only by the awareness that only the smallest part of classical culture had been reclaimed; the vast bulk, it was realised, had been lost for ever. But what remained had a profound impact upon the Renaissance.

That impact was physical, as well as aesthetic. In his *Renaissance Discovery of Classical Antiquity,* Roberto Weiss points to the importance of ancient remains in Italy in evoking a sense of interest in and respect for antiquity. The writers of the Middle Ages treated ancient remains chiefly as convenient landmarks to guide travellers on their search for famous churches or collections of relics, or as a cheap source of high-quality building materials. There was no real interest in the past associations of these imposing artifacts; their value lay entirely in their present utility. In the Renaissance, however, a new sense of historical empathy can be seen developing: ancient remains provided a point of contact with classical civilisation and culture. They were a concrete stimulus to reflection on the continuity of the historical process and the possible present value of the past. The spirit of Rome could be recaptured by walking through its ruins, by reading its literature and by mastering its language. The growing interest in historical investigation of both artifacts and documents, and awareness of the importance of evidence in historical reconstruction, led to a growing interest in the exploration of the past, and contains the germs of modern archaeology. The fifteenth- and sixteenth-centuries' debates over which modern Italian river corresponded to the Rubicon crossed by Caesar – the Fiumicino, the Pisciatello and the Uso being the most frequently mentioned possibilities – illustrates this development. The past was physically present, whether in the ever-present ruins of classical Rome, or in the ancient artifacts unearthed by builders, treasure-hunters and amateur archaeologists (such as the practically intact body of a Roman girl found in a sarcophagus on 19 April 1485).

During his first visit to Rome in the spring of 1337, the Renaissance poet Petrarch took the opportunity to wander among the ruins of the ancient city with his travelling companion Giovanni Colonna, armed with the best guide book available. In a letter written to Colonna a few weeks later, Petrarch re-lived the wonder and awe that he felt in the presence of ancient Rome, his imagination stirred by memories of Virgil and Livy. Petrarch's sense of historical and cultural empathy with ancient Rome captured the imagination of many in the fourteenth century, as may be seen from the paintings of the Paduan school of the period.

The Renaissance saw itself as heir to the riches of the classical period. It viewed itself as solemnly charged with responsibility for transforming the poverty of its own times with the cultural splendours of classical antiquity. Classical culture was not dead; it was a present living possibility. What was needed was a willingness to allow this classical paradigm to transform the present. It was this cultural programme which lay behind the slogan *ad fontes*.

The past was, however, seen as more than the source of artistic stimulus. It was also seen as setting patterns in history which could cast light on the present. Coluccio Salutati stated this point clearly: 'If one were to search diligently throughout history, one would plainly see the same cyclical pattern in human affairs, where although nothing recurs which is exactly the same, nevertheless every day we see a sort of image of past events renewed.' The history of classical Rome was therefore seen as having the potential to cast light on the present. It was an aid to interpreting historical developments and possibilities at the time of the Renaissance.

For the great city-states of the Italian Renaissance, such as Florence, the story of classical Rome provided a model which cast light on their situation. The Italian heirs to the classical period could expect echoes of its history to be discerned within their own. The shadows of contemporary history were illuminated by the story of ancient Rome. The 'there and then' of the past could easily elucidate the 'here and now' of the present.

This sense of solidarity with the classical period was of great importance to many sixteenth-century communities, which felt that their existence was threatened by political and military forces outside their control. One example of especial importance might be noted. In 1494, the French king Charles VII invaded northern Italy. Shock-waves resonated throughout the region. The sophisticated cultures of Italian cities such as Florence, developed during the high noon of the Italian Renaissance, seemed to be threatened with extinction. As Machiavelli – sometime Florentine representative at the French court – gloomily observed, culture seemed powerless as a defence against brute force.

A community under threat has a strong tendency to close ranks, and rediscover and reassert its identity. This is precisely what happened during the period. Florence laid even greater emphasis than usual on its connections with ancient Rome, apparently believing that this would stiffen the resolve of its citizens to resist the French. Would Florence be allowed to suffer the fate of ancient Rome – to be sacked by barbarians? The unthinkable could only be prevented by communal solidarity – which the links with ancient Rome served to strengthen.

A similar situation existed within the Swiss Confederation in the early sixteenth century, especially in the aftermath of the disastrous defeat of the Swiss at Marignano (1515). It was, of course, this event which led to the Swiss decision henceforth to remain neutral from all further international conflicts. The Swiss Confederation – a fragile political and cultural entity, even at the best of times – felt its existence was threatened by outside elements, and supplemented its military defences by the vigorous development of a cultural programme. The Swiss humanists (in marked contrast to Erasmus of Rotterdam, who regarded national identities and languages as outmoded) were committed to a nationalist vision, by which Swiss national identity was affirmed and sustained by the republic of letters. One of the more important ways of affirming this sense of national identity was through retelling stories of the formative period of the Confederation. By far the most celebrated of these narratives is the legend of William Tell, which assumed its definitive form in 1512, and rapidly assumed the status of a national myth. The story of William Tell identified the key values of the Swiss Confederation. It told of how heroically they had been defended in the past. It emphasised how important and worthwhile they were. And finally it implied that they were worth defending in the modern period. By being reminded of the roots of Swiss values, the successors of William Tell were being invited to renew, reaffirm and defend them in the modern period. Yet this is not something restricted to the world of the Italian Renaissance or the European Reformation; it remains of vital importance to the modern period. We can illustrate this by looking at its significance for modern western culture, taking as a particular example the case of the modern United States of America.

Reclaiming Roots in Modern Culture: The United States

The history of the United States of America shows up a phenomenon of central importance to Reformation spirituality. Roots matter to people – especially to people exiled from their homeland. Ethnic groupings, faced with the threat of being overwhelmed by a larger, more amorphous culture, choose to resist this development. How? By asserting their distinctiveness. And that distinctiveness is often specifically linked with an appeal to the past. To lose one's distinctiveness is to lose something irreplaceable and identity-giving, evoking a sense of loss of place and purpose in the world.

In a fine essay entitled 'The Southern Recovery of Memory and History', the noted American literary critic Lewis Simpson points to the enormous appeal of the vision of an idealised pastoral Old South to many modern southerners, alienated by the growing industrialisation of their region. The roots of their culture, conveniently divested of its associations with slavery, were seen to lie in a green and pleasant land, untainted by the industrialisation so characteristic of the despised North. As Simpson points out, a sense of having been expelled from Eden, of having lost a vital connection with an identity-giving past, pervades much literature of the south, such as the novels of William Faulkner. A feeling of alienation resulted in a new concern to trace one's roots, with a view to recovering that cultural oasis in the midst of a barren and sterile society. The past could live on in the present, through a recovery of cultural roots. As Faulkner asserted this principle: 'There is no such thing really as was, because the past is.'

This general phenomenon can be traced throughout modern America. Irish-Americans, anxious to preserve their cultural identity, celebrate their Irish roots with a degree of commitment and enthusiasm which is always something of a mystery to those who chose to stay behind in Ireland. Many recent American presidents have found it to be electorally important to discover that they have links – however distant – with the Emerald Isle. St Patrick's Day is celebrated with far greater fervour in New York than it is in Dublin. Why? Because it preserves the identity of a group which would otherwise lose its distinctive character. The same is true of the American Jewish community, which finds in the Passover celebrations a focus for its sense of identity. The new interest in the rediscovery of the African roots of black American culture is yet another illustration of this general principle of a return to cultural roots. Alex Haley's novel of the 1970s, *Roots*, made a deep and emotive appeal to this same sense of being rooted in the past. The recollection of past roots aids the preservation of present individuality. Who you are is partly determined by where you come from.

Lewis Simpson has written of modern America as a world of rootless and isolated consciousness in which 'the covenant with memory and history has been abrogated in favour of the existential self.' It is perhaps this factor which explains the remarkable appeal to many modern Americans of Garrison Keillor's fictional small town of Lake Wobegon. In his radio shows of the 1980s, Keillor touched deeply on the American sense of needing images of belonging, of connecting up with others, of sharing memories, of dwelling together in integrity, of staying together with commitment. Lake Wobegon is a place where people have put down roots, and feel they belong. The sociologists tell us that this is precisely where modern America is *not* – but the cultural analysts tell us that this is where a lot of modern America would like to be.

Individuals and society need to put down roots, to achieve both social and spiritual stability. People need to feel that they belong. It is perhaps no accident that the most bizarre recent religious cults generally have their origins in California, where a deep sense of rootlessness often prevails. Kids get involved with gangs because it gives them a sense of belonging somewhere. They have family problems, problems at school, and they feel they have been rejected by society – yet they belong in their gangs.

Let me develop this point in a slightly different direction. When a group feels itself to be under threat, it makes efforts to safeguard its cultural individuality. That danger may take several forms. It may be that the grouping feels that it will simply be absorbed within a greater whole, as when a small family company loses its identity through being taken over by a vast industrial conglomerate. This is certainly the case with Irish groups in North America. Or it may be that the grouping is being actively persecuted by those who have a vested interest in eliminating them, a situation faced by Jews in Europe in the 1930s and 1940s. But whether the threat is seen to be active or passive, whether it is real or imagined, the effect is much the same: the group closes ranks in an effort to preserve its distinctive outlook. To fail to do so is to risk merging into the cultural background, and losing sight of the tradition which has nourished and sustained that group until now.

Many American political and social writers of the 1960s spoke of the emergence of a multicultural society. By this, they appear to have meant that society was something like a melting pot, with its various cultural ingredients fused together to yield a monolithic and uniform product. Their individual identities were sacrificed in order to give a uniform multicultural entity. The imagery has now changed; a tossed salad has become a more acceptable way of reflecting contemporary cultural sensitivities. It has become abundantly clear that ethnic groups are proud of their cultures and their traditions, and have little interest in the idea of being submerged within an amorphous – and, it must be said, largely artificial – uniform global culture.

If the 'melting pot' imagery were sustained, the quest for cultural roots would become at best an irrelevance, at worst an impediment to the creation of a genuinely integrated multicultural society. But with the entirely wise abandonment of this utopian image, a more realistic and acceptable approach has begun to emerge. Each culture makes its own individual and unique contribution to the greater culture of which it has become part. The need to retain identity which this model presupposes involves a careful and deliberate recollection of the roots of such cultures, in order that their individuality and identity may be maintained.

This, then, illustrates the importance of the theme 'searching for roots' to Renaissance and modern American culture. To find one's roots is to gain insights into where we have come from. It is to gain some understanding of our present situation. It is to bring the cultural riches of the past in an acceptable form into the poverty of the present. And it is to gain a glimpse of future goals. It is to define a horizon, which is to be correlated with that of our own horizon. It is the task of the historian and others to allow these horizons to be fused, so that the relevance of the past for the present can be discerned. To discover one's roots is to gain a sense of continuity, belonging and identity; it is to locate oneself firmly in history; and it is to discover the possibility of support and solidarity with others who share the same roots.

I have spent some time talking in general terms about the importance of the past, and its identity-giving and identity-enhancing potential, using modern America and the Italian Renaissance as case studies. I think that I have now laid the ground for understanding this vital aspect of Reformation spirituality – the need to be refreshed and challenged by the past.

Precisely such a quest for roots lies at the heart of Reformation spirituality. One could designate the Reformation as being 'a quest for the authentic roots of faith'. For the reformers, the church can only remain faithful to its purpose and calling by recollecting – in the dual sense of 'remembering' and 'picking up again' – its origins. In this respect, Reformation spirituality echoes one of the deepest and most powerful themes of the European Renaissance – the great watchcry, *ad fontes* – 'back to the sources'.

Returning to the Roots of Faith

A central theme of Reformation spirituality is that the church lost its way during the Middle Ages. It was a time when the traditional concerns of the church became overwhelmed by the involvement of the church in the secular order. In our own day and age, such involvement is generally held to be an excellent and desirable thing. The history of the church during the Middle Ages, however, perhaps sounds a note of caution, indicating what can happen through over-extension of resources and personal commitment to the world. During the Middle Ages, the papacy saw its secular powers reach new heights. The ecclesiastical banking system came close to being the medieval equivalent of a modern multinational corporation. Indeed, the pope who condemned Martin Luther in 1520 was a prominent member of the Florentine Medici family, who had bought the papacy outright over the heads of a number of more distinguished and eligible rivals.

But in the middle of this experimentation with political and financial power, there were signs of decay. The arteries of the church became hardened through over-involvement in the world. A price was paid for this apparent success. What, it was increasingly asked, have the splendours of the Renaissance papacy to do with the humble figure of Jesus of Nazareth? There was a widespread perception within the church, often at high levels, that a redefinition of its aims and goals was required. A new model was needed. And for many – including those who would become the proponents of the Reformation – that model lay with the early church, as it can be seen emerging in the New Testament.

It was necessary to judge the modern church in the light of its origins. And just as Renaissance writers attempted to fuse the horizons of the classical period with the fifteenth century, so the reformers attempted such a fusion with the horizons of the New Testament and the sixteenth. By returning to the foundational events of the Christian church, it was argued, it was possible to recover the authentic roots of the Christian faith. A stream was purest at its source; rather than gulp the muddied and stagnant waters of the late medieval church, it was possible to sip the pure and fresh spring of the days of Christianity's youth.

It was a powerful vision. It was not, to be sure, a new vision. Monastic writers of twelfth-century France had shared it, as would the writers of the Oxford Movement in Victorian

England. But it made available a credible alternative to the questionable methods and goals of the late medieval church. The Renaissance had already developed, and given intellectual and cultural credibility to, the idea of a return to the sources of civilisation, in order that its modern successors might relearn its art. Why should not Christians return to the cradle of their faith, and allow its foundational events to impact upon their imaginations?

Scripture was thus read with a new sense of anticipation, with heightened expectations of what might be possible as a consequence. Behind the text there was an experience – the experience of a transformative encounter with the risen Christ, an experience long held to be absent from the corporate memory of the church. Zwingli and his circle wrote prophetically of *Christianismus renascens*, a Christianity being born all over again, through a return to the roots of faith. The recovery of memory and history was one component of this development; another was a grim determination to confront the church of the present with the remembrance – forgotten or repressed? – of a very different church. As a lover might confront his beloved with the love-letters of the days of their courtship in order to revitalise their languishing relationship, so the reformers hoped that the memory of another period in the life of the church might bring new life and fire to its fading embers. To return to Scripture was to renew a broken contract with memory and tradition, recognising in it the constitutive realm of religious being. The past was to be permitted to judge and condemn the present, before offering new possibilities for revitalisation and renewal.

It is true that the reformers returned to their scriptural roots with very different expectations. Luther was concerned to allow the crucified Christ, known only through Scripture, to challenge the theology and spirituality of the medieval church. Zwingli was concerned with the idea of ethical and religious solidarity with the early community of faith. And Calvin seems to have thought it possible to recreate in his own day and age the church structures of the apostolic period. But the common thread of continuity underlies them all. To return to one's roots is to recollect one's birthright. It is to regain the title deeds of faith. It is to catch a fresh vision of possibilities. It is to overhear the conversations of the apostles. It is to allow a tired and weary faith to be refreshed. It is to return to an oasis from which the pilgrimage into the wilderness was begun. And it was to ignite a powder-keg under the comfortable yet stagnant certainties of late medieval religion.

This, then, is the general strategy. But how was it pursued? And what was achieved by doing so? Another case study may be helpful, to indicate how one reformer aimed to present afresh to his own day a foundational event of the Christian faith – the death of Christ on the cross at Calvary.

Recalling the Roots of the Christian Community: The Eucharist

Earlier, I noted the importance of the appeal to the story of the past for both Renaissance Florence and the early Swiss Confederation. It is against this background that Zwingli's theory of the Lord's Supper or eucharist is to be set. (I shall use the term 'eucharist' to refer to this sacrament; Zwingli himself prefers to use terms such as 'remembrance', 'memorial', or 'supper'.) Zwingli affirms that the eucharist tells the story of the foundational event of the Christian community. By doing this, he argues, it gives substance to the values and aspirations of that community, and enhances its sense of unity and purpose.

Zwingli makes an explicit comparison between the death and resurrection of Jesus Christ and the foundational events of the Swiss Confederation. The Confederation is usually regarded as having secured its continued existence through the decisive defeat of its chief oppressor – the Austrians – in 1388 at the battle of Nahenfels. During this battle, the soldiers of the three original cantons wore white crosses on their tunic sleeves to identify their common loyalty – a feature now incorporated into the Swiss national flag. In that they came from three quite different locations, the soldiers might fail to recognise their common cause; the white cross ensured that they recognised that they were on the same side, avoiding embarrassing mix-ups.

So important was this victory that it was celebrated through an annual pilgrimage to the battle site. This became an important element in the fostering of a sense of national identity. The Swiss cantons (there were twelve in Zwingli's day) led virtually independent existences; there was a real danger that they might lose sight of their common Swiss allegiance. The pilgrimage was an annual occasion on which this loyalty could be renewed, as representatives of each of the cantons met together to recall how their solidarity had safeguarded their freedom in the past – and affirm that their future liberty depended upon maintaining their alliance.

Drawing on this as an analogy, Zwingli writes:

> If a man sews on a white cross, he proclaims that he wishes to be a confederate. And if he makes the pilgrimage to Nahenfels and gives God praise and thanksgiving for the victory vouchsafed to our forefathers, he testifies that he is a confederate indeed. Similarly, the man who receives the mark of baptism is the one who is resolved to hear what God says to him, to learn the divine precepts, and to live his life in accordance with them. And the man who in the remembrance or supper gives thanks to God in the congregation testifies to the fact that from the very heart he rejoices in the death of Christ, and thanks him for it.

Zwingli makes two points. First, the Swiss soldier wears a white cross as a token of allegiance, demonstrating publicly his loyalty to the Confederacy and all it stands for. It is an affirmation of solidarity with the community – including its values and aspirations – which was brought into existence through the events of Nahenfels. Similarly, the Christian demonstrates allegiance to the church publicly by attending the eucharist. It is an act of affirmation, in which believers affirm their solidarity with the community of faith, including its values and aspirations.

Second, the historical event which brought the Confederacy into being is recalled as a token of allegiance. The story of Nahenfels is retold, and its contemporary significance affirmed. That story is charged with values, which the resulting community is expected to maintain. It is this story which keeps the community together, setting its common goal. (Modern management studies have stressed the importance of agreement on goals for the cohesion of a corporation; there is an important parallel here for the Christian church.) This point is made particularly clearly, for example, by the highly politicised drama *The Old and the Young Confederates* (1516), which identifies Confederate values and affirms their importance in the aftermath of the disaster at Marignano. Similarly, the Christian commemorates the historical event which brought the Christian church into being and shaped its value- and belief-systems, as a token of commitment to that church. The eucharist is thus a memorial of the historical event leading to the establishment of the Christian church, and a public demonstration of the believer's allegiance to that church, its members and its values.

Recalling the death of Christ binds Christians together. That, in a nutshell, is one of the central features of Zwingli's understanding of the purpose of the eucharist It is a public demonstration of the mutual commitment of believers. It affirms the bond which holds them together – with each other on the one hand, and with the death of Jesus Christ on the other. A similar point is made by Oecolampadius, in his *Exposition of the True Words* (1525). The cup of wine, which is 'drunk with thanksgiving in memory of the death of Christ' has the vital function of reminding us of the shedding of the blood of Christ, and thus of 'uniting into one society all of us who believe that we have been redeemed by that blood'. (Significantly, Oecolampadius uses the Latin term *confederans* to refer to this process of 'binding together' – precisely the same term used to refer to the union of the Swiss Confederacy.)

The eucharist thus represents a return to Christian roots – to recall, and to recollect, the importance of the death of Jesus Christ for the life of the believer and the church. Here, it affirms, is the source of the church. Here, it declares, is the origin of Christian identity and mission. And to here, it proclaims, the church must return, to remember why it exists in the world in the first place. By reflecting upon the cost of its redemption, the church is enabled to gain a sense of perspective which would otherwise be missing. Christianity without the cross is not worthy of that name. What brought Christians together, and what holds Christians together, is the death of Christ. To substitute any other bond of common allegiance for this is to lose sight of the reason for the existence of the church – to proclaim Christ until he comes again. For Zwingli, the return to Christian roots is the prerequisite for the recovery of Christian identity.

Let us return briefly to the Italian Renaissance. As I pointed out earlier, the presence of the remains of ancient Roman buildings provided a powerful stimulus to the thinkers of the Renaissance. Here were visible and tangible reminders of the past – a past which could still shape the present. Zwingli treats the eucharist in much the same way. It evokes memories. It is a visible and tangible reminder of past roots – and is thus simultaneously a challenge to reappropriate them. It is to tell the story of the Christian faith, and rediscover what it means to be a believer. Just as the Old Testament constantly reminded Israel to remember her history – how God created, called and sustained her as a people – so Christians need to learn the story of how they were brought into being.

I once heard a professor of literature describe the importance of discovering one's story. This professor, who taught at a leading university in Southern California, was a Kiowa Indian, a native American from the Oklahoma region. He told us how he learned the story of his people as a boy. One day, just after dawn, his father woke him, and took him to the home of an elderly squaw. He left him there, promising to return to collect him that afternoon.

All that day, the squaw told this young boy the story of the Kiowa people. She told him of their origins by the Yellowstone River, and how they then migrated southward. She told him of the many hardships they faced – the wars with other Indian nations and the great blizzards on the winter plains. She told him of the glories of the life of the Kiowa nation – of the great buffalo hunts, the taming of wild horses, and the great skill of the braves as riders. Finally, she told him of the coming of the white man. She told him about the humiliation of their once-proud nation at the hands of the white soldiers, who forced them to move south to Kansas, where they faced starvation and poverty. Her story ended as she told him of their final humiliating confinement within a reservation in Oklahoma.

Shortly before dark, his father returned to collect him. His words about leaving the home of the squaw remain firmly planted in my mind. 'When I left that house, I was a Kiowa.' He had learned the story of his people, to which he was heir. He knew what his people had been through. Before he had learned that story, he had been a Kiowa in name only; now he was a Kiowa in reality.

Zwingli's approach is like that of the Kiowa squaw. He suggests that we see the eucharist as telling the story of the Christian people. He invites us to consider the eucharist as the powerful and evocative recollection of the foundational narrative of a community which is aware of its need to affirm its identity and relevance in the world. The eucharist provides us with a lens, through which the scriptural narrative of the death of Jesus may be read. It provides a focus of identity for the Christian community. It affirms that this is *our* story. It declares that we *belong* to this story. It asserts that the community of faith, and its individual members, possess deep and stable roots, firmly grounded in the history of the world. To be a Christian is to matter – and to belong. No matter how unstable the society or culture in which Christians may find themselves, they may rest assured of their stability. Their identity is *given*; it needs to be rediscovered and repossessed.

Conclusion

In this chapter, I have been exploring the potential of returning to the past for Christian spirituality. It has been the general method, rather than specific approaches, which has been my central concern, although I hope the case study above illustrates the richness and sophistication which came readily to the reformers as they sought to make present the past. For the reformers, the past possesses a capacity to illuminate, interpret – and even to transform – the present. The relevance of the crucifixion lies not in the fact that it is past, but that it is foundational, charged with interpretative and existential power.

Let me invite you to consider once more Renaissance Italy. The Renaissance was a period of perhaps unparalleled creativity in European culture. It seemed to breathe new life and fresh vitality into the life of humanity. Yet, as Roberto Weiss suggests, this came about through both a physical and a cultural encounter with the past. The past breathed fresh air into the stagnant atmosphere of medieval Europe. Through wrestling with this cultural heritage, a period of outstanding creativity and originality dawned. The same is true of other periods. An excellent example might be the Oxford Movement within the Church of England, which traces its origins to 1833.

The Oxford Movement drew its inspiration from the apostolic church. The critical comparison between the contemporary and actual church of the nineteenth century with the historic and ideal church of the apostles proved to be enormously creative, providing a stimulus to development and innovation which led to what can only be described as a renaissance in religious life in England and far beyond. The vitality and life of that movement was due to a willingness to allow the present to be challenged and nourished by its historical roots. Past roots contributed a powerful impetus to present reflection and recollection, and future transformation.

There is a theological parallel here for our own day and age. I do not wish to labour this point; it is perhaps too evident to require me to do so. Yet it seems to me, as it seems to many others, that the most exciting things happening in the fields of Christian theology and spirituality today involve a willingness and an ability to engage with the central and foundational resources of the Christian faith – the cross and resurrection of Jesus Christ. And that is certainly the direction in which Reformation spirituality is pointing us, urging us to achieve a fusion of the horizons of the past and present.

But let me return to this sense of rootlessness which is characteristic of much North American – not to mention Australasian – society today. There is a need for individuals and their communities to gain a sense of being rooted, of belonging, of having continuity with the past. The great Old Testament theme of 'looking to the rock from which you were hewn' suggests itself.

The Christian believer and the Christian community may – and must – recover a sense of belonging, of having deep spiritual roots, even in the midst of a new, young and immature society. To be a Christian is to trace one's roots back two millennia, to the great events of the first Good Friday and Easter Day. It is to renew the covenant with memory and history. It is to recover the sense of *belonging* in history, however fractured the social location of one's life may be. In short: it is to put down roots, no matter how shallow the soil of life.

Roots are important for continuity and stability; they nurture the conditions under which growth and maturity may develop. Tradition encourages wariness, through exercising a restraining influence upon innovation. An enduring tradition, firmly located in history and taken seriously by those who claim to be its heirs, ensures caution and continuity within that community. Faithfulness to one's roots is not inconsistent with addressing contemporary needs and opportunities. At first sight, this respect for roots might seem to be a recipe for encouraging unoriginality and the stifling of creativity. But there is another side to this story. Commitment to a tradition is not equivalent to an encrusted dogmatism, a denial of the freedom to think or of the importance of creativity. Freedom to think without an accompanying commitment to a tradition can lead to little more than an unanchored chaos. The twentieth century has provided us with ample historical examples of what happens when a society breaks free from the restraining force of tradition. Nazi Germany and the Stalinist Soviet Union are excellent illustrations of the unacceptable consequences of a break with tradition. Walter Benjamin's *Theses on the Philosophy of History* reflect his despair at the totalitarianism which results when a civilised society chooses to break with its traditional values. It is very easy to break with one's roots; but, as the cultural history of the Soviet Union in recent years makes clear, it is very difficult to pick up those roots, once broken.

And, as history also makes clear, such radical breaks with tradition tend to be short-lived, experiments in politics and theology which rarely last more than a generation. The French Revolution, whose consequences are still with us, might be cited as a counter-argument to this suggestion – but that Revolution saw itself as reclaiming the traditional classic notion of republicanism, as embodied in the Roman republic. Its methods might be revolutionary; its goals were altogether traditional. The paradox of that revolution is that, while it used thoroughly revolutionary means to achieve its ends, the ends it chose to achieve were thoroughly traditional. I must confess that, having studied the history of western culture in some depth, I have come to the conclusion that tradition is what keeps ideas alive.

Finally, let me turn to one aspect of the Reformation search for Christian roots which has new importance today. The modern period has seen a renewed interest in the whole area of Christian unity. Our exploration of this component of Reformation spirituality allows us to make a daring, radical and exciting step – to suggest that we return directly to the source of faith, to re-experience and recapture its vitality, and bring into the modern age that faith to which every page of the New Testament bears such a vibrant witness. We need to return to the cross, and ponder its meaning for us and our situation today, without having to fight our way through the dividing and divisive centuries of disagreement. A filter has been placed between us and the cradle of faith, which it is necessary to remove. The Christian church must learn to return to where she once started from, in order that she may go forward into the future. The search for Christian unity is fundamentally a search for Christian roots. It is a return to the foot of the cross, to discover our faith all over again. It is a return to the Johannine upper room, to regain our vision and mission. In the famous words of T.S. Eliot:

> We shall not cease from exploration
> And the end of all our exploring
> Will be to arrive where we started
> And know the place for the first time.

Precisely this note is struck in what is possibly the most powerful spirituality of Christian roots to emerge from the sixteenth century – Luther's 'theology of the cross'.

4   The Dark Night of Faith: Luther's Theology of the Cross

Crux sola est nostra theologia. I shall never forget the first time I encountered those words of Martin Luther. I had arrived at Cambridge in 1978, fresh from the study of theology at Oxford, and had begun a process of total immersion in the theological literature of the Reformation. Having cut my theological teeth on Karl Barth, I decided to deepen my knowledge of two fundamental sources of modern religious thought – Martin Luther and John Calvin. It was during the spring of 1979 that I came across those words. They seemed to leap out of the page. 'The cross alone is our theology.' I stopped taking notes, and paused to think. Luther's declaration seemed electrifying, charged with power, potential and challenge.

It also seemed absurd. How could a past event have such present-day relevance? And why should it be *this* event? What conceivable justification could be given for this selective attention, this concentration upon the cross? To demonstrate how that focus arose within Luther's theology and spirituality was one thing; but how could the cross function as the core of Christian theology in a period dominated by the insights of the Enlightenment? Moulded as I then was by the English liberal theological tradition, I eventually dismissed Luther's approach as outdated and obsolete, of interest only to historians of doctrine and early Reformation theology. They could have no place in modern Christian thought. I resumed taking notes, and passed on.

Nevertheless, his words remained in my mind. Somehow, they seemed to capture something which I intuitively felt was indefinably wrong with the gentle theological liberalism with which I then identified. On looking back on the development of my thinking since then, Luther's brief phrase proved to be the rock on which my liberalism foundered. The 'theology of the cross', through which Luther challenged his own age to allow the cross of Christ to assume centre stage, proved able to challenge modernity.

Let us begin by setting this remarkable theology in its historical context. The years 1517 and 1519 are widely regarded as being of decisive importance to the Reformation. In 1517, Luther sparked off a furious theological storm with his Ninety-five Theses on indulgences. In 1519, he would become a *cause célèbre* on account of his powerful performance at the Leipzig Disputation. Pitted against John Eck, Luther challenged many of the traditional ideas of the medieval Catholic church, especially on papal authority. The debate he sparked off proved to have been instrumental in engendering the Reformation.

The year 1518, in contrast, was a quiet period. It is all too easy to pass it over as little more than an interval separating two pivotal events, a valley nestling between two mountains. Yet in April of that year, Luther was invited to preside over the traditional public disputation of the Augustinian Order at Heidelberg. It was his own religious order, and he was among friends. And it was in the course of this disputation that Luther put forward the 'theology of the cross'. Let me quote one of the most important statements which Luther makes:

> Anyone who looks upon the invisible things of God as they are seen in created things does not deserve to be called a theologian. Whoever sees the visible rearward parts of God, as seen in suffering and the cross, does deserve to be called a theologian.

For Luther, the cross is the centre of the Christian faith. The haunting image of the crucified Christ is the crucible in which all our thinking about God is forged. Luther expresses the centrality of the cross in a series of terse statements, such as 'The cross alone is our theology,' and 'The cross puts everything to the test.' He draws a now-famous distinction between the 'theologian of glory', who seeks God apart from Jesus Christ, and the 'theologian of the cross', who knows that God is revealed in and through the cross of Christ.

The Cross and the Critique of Reason

In what way is God revealed in the cross? In answering this question, Luther lays the foundation for his criticism of the role of reason in the Christian life. Christian spirituality and theology cannot rely upon reason as a resource. Luther's 'evangelical irrationalism' arises from his insistence that the cross discloses the limitations placed upon human reason. To understand his point, it is necessary to consider the notion of a *hidden revelation* of God in the cross. This is a difficult idea. However, once grasped, it is remarkably helpful in making sense of many enigmatic aspects of Christian existence and experience. One way of approaching it is to take up Luther's notion of the 'visible rearward parts of God', a curious phrase which is derived from Exodus 33:23. You will remember the context of that verse. Moses is not allowed to see the face of God; he catches an indirect glimpse of him, seen from the back, as God passes by. It really is God whom Moses sees; but he is not allowed to gain a direct sight of God's face.

So, Luther suggests, it is with us. The cross is like that revelation of God to Moses. It really is a revelation of God – but it is not immediately recognisable as such. But as we begin to reflect upon the cross, we begin to realise the wonder of what God has done. Here is God at work, as St Paul suggests, making mockery of the wisdom of the wise, and showing up the futility of human ideas of strength. God has shown up human wisdom in all its poverty for what it really is, by revealing himself in a scene of utter folly and weakness. Reason says: there is just no way that God could reveal himself like this! And thus reason shows how inept it is as a theological resource. By revealing himself in this way, God gently calls into question our natural tendency to rely on common sense to tell us about himself.

Again, common sense expects God to reveal himself in situations of great glory and power. The cross tells us that God chose to reveal himself in the cross of shame and weakness. Again, the reliability of our reason is called into question. We are being asked to learn the hardest lesson of Christian theology – the need to be humble, and accept God as he has revealed himself, rather than as we would like him to be. Luther puts this rather trenchantly:

> This is clear. Whoever does not know Christ does not know God hidden in suffering. Therefore he or she prefers works to suffering, glory to the cross, strength to weakness, wisdom to folly . . . These are the people who Paul calls 'the enemies of the cross', for they hate the cross and love works and the glory of works.

So a central theme of the 'theology of the cross' is the divine contradiction of the innate human tendency to devalue what the world regards as weak, foolish and humble – for it is through precisely these things that God has chosen to work.

The theology of the cross thus provides a foundation for Luther's critique of the role of reason in the Christian life. While Luther, as a medieval university professor, upholds the importance and value of human reason in virtually every area of Christian life, not least the academic life, he nevertheless insists that we shall be led astray if we rely upon it for our knowledge of God. The self-revelation of God provided at Calvary provides a powerful critique of purely rational approaches to theology. Reason suggests that God ought to reveal himself in such situations as the world accepts as great, majestic, glorious and powerful – whereas God has in fact chosen to reveal himself in a situation of tragedy, grief, despair and weakness. By doing so, Luther argues, God is gently pointing out the limitations of reason. We ought to attend to God as he actually is, rather than constructing ideas of how we would like him to be.

A firm emphasis upon the priority of God's self-revelation is easily discerned as underlying this understanding of the role of the cross in the Christian life. The self-revelation of God is a demand for self-humility on the part of the theologian. We must learn to respond to God. God has taken the initiative away from us, pulling the rug from under our neat preconceptions of what a god ought to be like. In part, faith is a willingness to apprehend and respond to God as he has chosen to make himself known. It is a form of humility (a characteristic emphasis for the young Luther), in that it amounts to a willingness to submit to God, rather than assert the validity of our own stereotypes of divinity (wherever these may have come from). True spirituality is not a human invention, but a response to God.

The Cross as the Criticism of Experience

If the cross represents a criticism of reason, it also mounts a powerful attack on another human resource upon which too much spiritual weight is often placed, especially in modern western thought. The experience of the individual is singled out as having revelatory authority. 'What I experience is what is right.' 'I don't experience it that way.' Luther suggests that individual experience is often seriously unreliable as a guide to matters of faith. The way we experience things isn't necessarily the way things really are.

An example – which I hasten to add is not used by Luther himself – might be helpful in bringing out the point at issue. Suppose you have been out of doors for some time on a very cold night. You arrive at the house of a friend, who notices how cold you are. 'What you need is a good drink,' he tells you. 'Have a glass of brandy.' You drink it. And after a few minutes, you become conscious of a feeling of warmth. You experience the brandy as having warmed you up.

But in fact, the brandy will make you colder. The alcohol causes your blood vessels to dilate, giving you the impression that your body is *producing* heat; in fact, it is *losing* heat. You may feel that you are warming up – but in reality, you are cooling down. Heat is being given off from your body, not taken in by it. Your feelings have led you seriously astray. Were you to drink alcohol to 'warm yourself up' in a bitterly cold situation, it is quite possible you could die from the resulting heat loss. An external observer would be able to detect what was really happening – but this perspective would be denied to you, to the extent that you relied upon your feelings.

This example has real spiritual relevance. It makes the point that experience needs to be *interpreted*. It needs to be *criticised*. You felt that you were being warmed up – but the correct interpretation of that experience is that you actually felt the heat *leaving* your body, to be radiated outward and lost to you. You need an external reference point by which those feelings can be evaluated and judged. Luther develops a related argument: our experiences of God need to be interpreted. The way we experience things isn't necessarily the way things really are. The cross provides an external reference point by which our feelings can be evaluated and judged.

Perhaps the best way to understand the spiritual importance of Luther's approach here is to consider the scene of helplessness and hopelessness on that first Good Friday, as Jesus Christ died upon the cross. The crowd gathering round the cross were expecting something dramatic to happen. If Jesus really was the son of God, they could expect God to intervene and rescue him. Yet, as that long day wore on, there was no sign of a dramatic divine intervention. In his cry from the cross, even Jesus himself experienced a momentary yet profound sense of the absence of God, 'My God, my God, why have you forsaken me?' Many expected God to intervene dramatically in the situation, to deliver the dying Jesus. But nothing of the kind happened. Jesus suffered, and finally died. There was no sign of God acting in that situation. So those who based their thinking about God solely on experience drew the obvious conclusion: God was not there.

The resurrection overturned that judgement. God was revealed as having been present and active at Calvary, working out the salvation of humanity and the vindication of Jesus Christ. He was not *perceived* to be present – but present he really was. What experience interpreted as the absence of God, the resurrection showed up as the *hidden presence* of God. God may have been experienced as inactive, yet the resurrection showed

God to have been active behind the scenes, working in secret. For Luther, the resurrection demonstrates how unreliable the verdict of human experience really is. Instead of relying upon the misleading impressions of human experience, we should trust in God's promises. God promises to be present with us, even in life's darkest hours – and if experience cannot detect him as being present, then that verdict of experience must be considered unreliable.

Luther suggests that we think of human existence as being like that first Good Friday. We see many things which puzzle and frighten us, and lead us to conclude that God is absent from or inactive in that situation. Suffering is an excellent example. How, we often wonder, can God be present in human suffering? Much the same thoughts must have passed through the minds of those watching Jesus Christ suffer and die. The first Easter Day, however, transformed that situation, and our understanding of the way in which God is present and active in his world. It showed that God is present and active in situations in which experience might indicate he is absent and inactive – such as suffering.

It is only when the experience of Good Friday is viewed in the light of the resurrection that the strange and mysterious manner in which God was at work can be discerned. The fundamental question raised by Good Friday is that raised earlier, and with such passion, by the Book of Job in the Old Testament – is God *really there*, amidst the contradictions of human experience? The resurrection speaks to us, as from a whirlwind, of the real and redeeming presence of God in situations from which he appears to be absent. Christian existence is life under the cross, life spent in its shadow while we await the dawn of the resurrection light. Christian faith begins where atheism supposes that it must be at an end – with the death of Jesus Christ.

The picture of God that is given to us by the cross is that of a deserted, bruised, bleeding and dying God, who lent new meaning and dignity to human suffering by passing through its shadow himself. God enters the world at the very point at which humanity is weak rather than strong, put to shame rather than proud. The darker and inevitable moments of life, culminating in pain, the knowledge of dying and death, are not areas of life from which God has been excluded, but areas in which he has deliberately included himself. The presence of God in the dark side of faith and life is given superb expression in Luther's famous statement, 'Abraham closed his eyes and hid himself in the darkness of faith – and found eternal light in its midst.' God himself chose this way – the way of darkness, dereliction and death – to redeem us from these, our last enemies. 'After Good Friday, humanity began to suffer in hope' (Leon Bloy). The powerful image of a God who knows what human suffering and pain are like, who *understands* at first hand what it is like to be weak, frail and mortal, is authorised by the cross of Jesus Christ.

According to Luther, we should apply such insights to our own situation. There are times when all of us find it difficult to accept that God is present and active – suffering being a case in point. If we try to think of these times in the light of Good Friday, we can see that those same thoughts and fears were expressed then. Yet the resurrection overturned those thoughts and fears, showing us how unreliable human experience is in these matters. Our present experience seems like Good Friday. God may not seem to be obviously present and active. But just as faith sees Good Friday from the standpoint of Easter Day, so it must also see the same patterns of interpretation in present experience. What *looks like* divine absence is really hidden divine presence.

This has important results for Luther's understanding of faith. Faith is an ability to see God's presence and activity in the world, and in our own experience. Faith sees behind external appearances and the misleading impressions of experience. It is an openness, a willingness, to find God where he has promised to be, even when experience suggests that he is not there. Luther uses the phrase 'the darkness of faith' to make this point. This has important results for Luther's understanding of the nature of doubt.

Doubt shows up our natural tendency to base our judgements upon experience, rather than faith. When faith and experience seem to be out of step with each other, we tend to trust our experience, rather than faith. But, Luther points out, how unreliable a guide experience turns out to be! Those who trusted in experience on the first Good Friday looked very foolish in the light of the resurrection! For Luther, the resurrection demonstrates the superiority of faith in the promises of God over reliance upon experience or reason. We must learn to let God be God, and trust in him and his promises, rather than in our own finite and inadequate perception of a situation.

The cross thus destroys our confidence in our own ability to discern what God is like. It shatters our misplaced trust in reason and experience to let us know who God is, and what he is like. It forces us to admit defeat, to concede our need to be told about God, instead of deciding in advance what he is like. By revealing himself through the suffering, weakness and shame of the cross, God forces us to abandon our preconceived ideas about him. God breaks down our preconceptions about him, so that we will be more willing to learn from him. Humility is essential, if we are to encounter and deepen our knowledge of the God who was present and active at Calvary.

Although Luther is critical of the role of experience in spirituality, he does not dismiss it as an irrelevance. Indeed, Luther insists that there is one experience which is basic to being a theologian. He describes this briefly in one of his most quoted (and most difficult!) statements. 'It is living, dying, and even being condemned which makes a theologian – not reading, speculating and understanding.' When I first read those words of Luther, I found them baffling. Surely theology was about reading Scripture, and trying to make sense of it? What was Luther complaining about? Now I know, and I am convinced that Luther is right. To be a *real* theologian is to wrestle with none other than the living God – not with ideas about God, but with God himself. And how can a sinner ever hope to deal adequately with this God?

If you want to be a real theologian, Luther insists, you must have experienced a sense of condemnation. You must have had a moment of insight, in which you realise just how sinful you really are, and how much you merit the condemnation of God. Christ's death on the cross spells out the full extent of

God's wrath against sin, and shows us up as sinners who are condemned. It is only from this point that we can fully appreciate the central theme of the New Testament – how God was able to deliver sinners from their fate. Without a full awareness of our sin, and the dreadful gulf this opens up between ourselves and God, we cannot appreciate the joy and wonder of the proclamation of forgiveness through Jesus Christ. In a letter to his colleague Philip Melanchthon, dated 13 January 1522, Luther suggested that he ask the so-called 'prophets' who were then confusing the faithful at Wittenberg the following question: 'Have they experienced spiritual distress and the divine birth, death and hell?' A list of spiritual sensations is no substitute for the terror that accompanies a real encounter with the living God. For these modern prophets, Luther wrote, 'the sign of the Son of man is missing'.

A modern illustration might make this point. In his book *The Restoring Word*, J. Randall Nichols wrote of an experience he had while visiting the Greek island of Corfu. 'Some of the most beautiful music I ever heard was the chanting of Greek peasant women, tears streaming down their lined and hardened faces, in a church on Corfu one Good Friday. I asked someone why they were weeping. "Because," he said, "their Christ is dead." I have often thought that I will never understand what resurrection means until I can weep like that.' Nichols' point, so memorably made, is that we can never appreciate the joy and hope of the resurrection, unless we have been plunged into the sense of hopelessness and helplessness which pervaded that first Good Friday. What is true of the resurrection is also true of forgiveness. Christian spirituality is grounded in an awareness of being a condemned sinner – an experience which is utterly transformed by divine forgiveness. We can never understand what forgiveness really means until we have wept the tears of condemnation.

Just about anyone can read the New Testament, and make some sort of sense of it. But, Luther insists, the *real* theologian is someone who has experienced a sense of condemnation on account of sin – who reads the New Testament, and realises that the message of forgiveness is good news for him or her. The gospel is thus experienced as something liberating, something which transforms our situation, something which is relevant to us. It is very easy to read the New Testament as if it were nothing more than any other piece of literature. And Luther reminds us that it is only through being aware of our sin, and all its implications, that we can fully appreciate the wonder of the electrifying declaration that God has forgiven our sins through Jesus Christ.

A similar point emerges during Luther's exposition of Romans (1515–16). It is possible to be a diligent scholar, Luther argues, and yet completely miss the point of the meaning of the New Testament.

> Great scholars who read a lot, and own lots of books, are not the best Christians . . . The best Christians are those who do from a free and willing heart what the scholars read about in books and teach others to do. We must therefore get worried when, in our own day and age, people become scholars through writing lots of books – but haven't the slightest idea what it means to be a Christian.

Luther may not have foreseen the academic and scholarly explosion of the modern period; nevertheless, he predicted with grim accuracy the problem which has resulted. The word 'theologian' has come to mean an academic professional, one whose credentials are established by his publication record. For Luther, that word was reserved for those who have experienced, and *know* they have experienced, the grace of the living God.

Luther's account of the relation between faith and experience is one of the most important and difficult aspects of his spirituality. It is remarkably helpful in beginning to think through questions such as the nature of doubt, and the way in which we detect God's presence and activity in the world, and in our own personal lives. But there is another aspect to this spirituality of the cross which is perhaps its most powerful feature. It centres on the Latin term *passio* – an ambiguous Latin term, which may bear the meaning 'suffering' or 'being acted upon'. Luther is concerned to stress the importance of both in the Christian spiritual life. Let us explore first the new value and dignity which Luther attaches to human suffering.

Suffering and Spirituality

'We would not be Christians if we did not suffer with Christ.' The cross stands as the final contradiction of those who proclaim that becoming a Christian involves an easy passage through life. In the midst of the euphoria surrounding the resurrection of Jesus, there was a real danger that Christian faith and existence would ascend to the heavens, finally abandoning any point of contact with the realities of this world. The New Testament makes no attempt to play down the importance of the resurrection of Christ for believers. But it quite deliberately directs our attention back to the cross. Believers must not allow their experiences of the risen Christ to distract them from the demands which their faith makes upon them here and now. The call to follow Jesus is a call to share in his sufferings (Mark 8:31–38), as well as in his risen glory. The pattern which believers learn to impose upon their existence is that of journeying *through* suffering, rejection and death *to* eternal life and the glory of the risen Christ. There is no manner in which these may be by-passed. They are the authentic marks of Christian spirituality.

These insights give added weight to the theology of the cross as it bears upon the experience of the individual believer. Suffering, humiliation and rejection are, in effect, the hallmarks of faith. They are the demonstration that believers are true disciples, the guarantee that they will share in the glory of the risen Christ. The cross thus lends new meaning to human suffering. Just as believers are baptised with the sign of the cross to signify that they are children of God, so the life of every child of God is shaped and influenced by the suffering and cross of Jesus Christ. 'The real and true work of the passion of Christ is to conform us to Christ.' Baptism does not merely stand at the beginning of the Christian life – it symbolises the whole of that life, a constant dying and rising with Christ. Just as Christ was 'handed over' to suffering, so

Christians are 'handed over' in the same way. By recognising the pattern of the cross – through suffering to glory – in their own experience, believers know that they stand within the promises of God, that they are sharing in the paschal mystery, that they are heirs to the riches of Christ. 'Wherever Christ is, it is inevitable that Judas, Pilate, Herod, Caiaphas and Annas will be there as well, with the cross thrown in for good measure.'

Luther's stress upon the cruciform pattern of the Christian life is open to a serious misunderstanding. Consider a passage such as the following: 'Anyone who is not *crucianus* (if I might coin a word) is not *Christianus*. In other words, anyone who does not bear his cross is no Christian, because he is not like his master, Jesus Christ.' This might be taken to suggest a spirituality of mimesis, of human imitation of the example of Jesus – a very medieval notion, firmly grounded in, for example, the writings of Thomas à Kempis. Luther's point is actually very different. It is that the true Christian is conformed to the likeness of Christ (note the use of a passive, rather than active, verb). Faith is not a human activity which seeks to imitate Christ, in an external manner; rather, faith is the means by which God is enabled to conform us to Christ. Luther's idea of 'being conformed to Christ' is an assertion of divine activity within us, not of self-sustaining human imitation of Christ. '"Being conformed to Christ" is not something that we can achieve by our own powers. It is the gift of God, not our own work.' As Luther stresses, to become a Christian is not to seek suffering, nor actively to imitate the suffering of Christ; rather it is to allow God to conform us to Christ, to become a participator in the suffering of Christ.

It is for this reason that Luther emphasises, perhaps to the astonishment of his contemporaries, the positive spiritual aspects of suffering. Where other theologians might try to defend the honour of God, or argue that suffering is necessary to make this a good world, or that evil is really good, Luther addresses directly the spiritual bewilderment and anguish of those who are suffering. The following passage is directly addressed to those who suffer:

A theologian of the cross (that is, one who speaks of the crucified and hidden God) teaches that suffering, the cross and death are the most precious treasure of all, and the most sacred relics which the Lord of this theology has himself consecrated and blessed, not just by the touch of his most holy flesh, but also by the embrace of his most holy and divine will. And he has left these relics here to be kissed, sought after, and embraced. How fortunate and blessed is anyone who is considered by God to be so worthy that these treasures of Christ should be given to him!

Suffering and faith belong together, and are directly related in their intensity and quality.

But this is not to say that Luther is some form of spiritual masochist, suggesting that believers should flagellate themselves, literally or metaphorically. 'If we are to suffer, then let it be suffering which God imposes upon us, not suffering which we choose to impose upon ourselves. For God knows best what suffering will help and serve us.' In other words, the Christian is to wait upon God, to see whether suffering will come his way, and what form it will take. (Note, incidentally, the close link between the two senses of *passio* in this citation.) Suffering is not something we need seek out, or impose upon ourselves. The true Christian is one who is aware of the inevitability of cruciform suffering in the life of faith, and is content to leave to God its place, time and nature.

For Luther, the believer and Christ are united in a close union by faith, the believer sharing in the life of Christ, and Christ in the life of the believer. Faith is like a marriage contract, leading to the mutual sharing of goods between the believer and Jesus Christ. What is ours (sin and death) becomes his, and what is his (salvation and life) becomes ours. The life of Christ breaks through into that of the believer in this 'marvellous exchange' (*commercium admirabile*). And the riches, the heritage, which Christ bestows upon us is the privilege of suffering with him, in order that we may be raised with him; of treading the same path as he once trod, leading first to the cross, and then to glory.

It is here that faith is put to the test: does glory really lie beyond the cross? Does the cross mark the end of life, or its beginning? The life of faith is a life lived in the firm and steadfast conviction that the cross is the only gate to glory, that it is the only entrance to the New Jerusalem, and that the suffering, pain and contradictions of our life as believers will be resolved and transformed, just as Good Friday gave way to Easter Day. We may see darkly now, as through some dark and opaque glass; on the final day, we shall see things as they really are.

Without the resurrection, the way of the cross would be little more than ascetic self-denial, at best a way of resignation to the futility of existence, at worst a way of despair and delusion. It is faith in the resurrection of Jesus Christ, and the recognition of its implications for our own existence, which gives the theology of the cross its sense of realism and purpose. To walk on this road is to walk the way of suffering, pain and rejection which leads only to the cross – but faith recognises that we pass through the cross to greet the one who has already passed through it before us, and awaits us on the other side.

What are the spiritual implications of this in the modern period? As writers such as Jürgen Moltmann have shown, Luther's ideas have power and relevance to all who are oppressed, poor and suffering. Indeed, the very title of Moltmann's most important book, *The Crucified God*, is a direct quotation from Luther. Luther's theology of the cross speaks of God's solidarity with the downtrodden, the suffering – indeed, with all that the world rejects as weak, foolish, and irrelevant. The cross is the affirmation that God accepts what we reject – a powerful challenge to our own standards of judgement. Let Luther have the final word on this point.

> It is the poor and the suffering who belong to the kingdom of Christ. It was for their sake that this king came down from heaven to earth. So his kingdom is for those who live in fear, sorrow and misery. To such I now preach, just as the angel preached to the poor, frightened shepherds: 'Behold, I bring you good news of great joy!'

But let me now turn to this second aspect of *passio*. One of the most characteristic features of Luther's spirituality is his criticism of human activism and achievement-orientated religion. Luther's criticism of human 'works' (*opera*) is very easily mis-understood. We may illustrate this from a phrase which occurs in Thesis 21 of the Heidelberg Disputation. Luther here declares that the person who 'does not know Christ' prefers 'works to suffering'. Although there is a definite *double entendre* here, the English translation misses the full sense of Luther's point. The person Luther is criticising is one who relies upon his own resources; who has failed to grasp that our 'actions', 'activities' or 'efforts' (to use some words which capture the sense of Luther's text far better than the leaden term 'works') fail to deliver the spiritual goods; who has yet to discover what it means and what it implies to allow God to act upon us.

Luther does not make this point, but it seems fair to note it in this connection. The passion narratives of the Gospels do indeed centre upon the *suffering* of Jesus – but they also centre on the fact that *things are being done* to Jesus. In the accounts of Jesus' ministry, Jesus is acting. He does things. Verbs which concern him are active. But in the accounts of his passion, a dramatic shift occurs. Things are done to Jesus. Verbs which concern him are passive. By placing stress upon the passion of Christ, Luther is implying that this same pattern of divine passion shapes the Christian existence. In matters of faith, it is God who acts, and the believer who is acted upon.

The tranquillity of faith – so powerful a theme of Luther's spirituality – rests upon recognising that *God* has done all that is necessary for our salvation in Jesus Christ, and has done it well. We are asked to accept what God has done for us in Jesus Christ, and act upon it. True peace is not an absence of problems; it is an ability to trust in God in their midst.

> The person who has peace is not someone who nobody troubles. That sort of peace is the peace that the world gives. Rather, it is the person who everybody afflicts and torments, and yet joyfully and quietly copes with them all.

'We must respond to Christ's passion, not with words or forms, but with life and truth' (Luther). The cross is not merely the source of ideas about God, but the basis of Christian existence. It stamps the form of the believer's existence, and establishes the cross as the natural pattern of Christian life. This idea is far removed from the notion that 'bearing our cross' is some form of meritorious work, which only the more spiritually enlightened believer need undertake. Precisely because the believer shares in Christ's passion, his existence is shaped by the cross. We could say that the cross of Christ is taken up in an existential manner by the believer. Anything which serves to detach the believer from the cross – whether material riches or spiritual pride – is a potential threat to the vitality and authenticity of his Christian life. 'The cross of Christ is nothing else than forsaking everything and clinging with the heart's faith to Christ alone' (Luther). The cross, with all that this entails, is laid upon the believer as part of his Christian life – and in recognising and accepting this fact, believers clinch their calling. We do not need to seek the cross, for we already stand under it. It is not something chosen by the believer – it is something which is imposed upon him or her through that very faith. The spiritual growth of the believer is largely concerned with the increasing recognition that his or her entire life is inextricably linked with the passion, death and resurrection of Jesus Christ, and thus *becoming* what he *already is*: 'The real and true work of the passion of Christ is to conform us to Christ' (Luther).

The Theology of the Cross – Today

So what might the modern relevance of this spirituality be? It is quite possible that the reader will have made many connections with the modern religious situation during the course of reading this chapter thus far. However, it may be helpful if I attempt to indicate some of the potential for this approach to help us deal with three important areas relating to modern spirituality.

First, Luther's theology of the cross poses a devastating challenge to what I shall call a 'what's-in-it-for-me?' spirituality. Many modern spiritualities are very human-centred, stressing their advantages for human mental health and wholeness. Their appeal is egocentric: adopt this spirituality, and you will have a better life. For Luther, one of the most important consequences of faith in Christ is participating in his sufferings. It is about being conformed to Christ – and that means that glory only comes through suffering. It is a strongly Christocentric spirituality: its appeal lies in the immense attractiveness of Jesus Christ, and the inherent *rightness* of being united to him. To be, or to become, a Christian is to do yourself no favours; it is simply to make the appropriate and the right response to what God has done for us in Christ. Luther's spirituality is profoundly moral, where many others are unashamedly directed towards the individual's self-satisfaction.

Second, if Luther is right, the 'health and wealth' gospel, which has had such influence in North America, would have to be called into question. A series of books with deeply revealing titles, such as 'God's Will is Prosperity', develop a spirituality which, while claiming to be Christian, has deeply secular roots. Their basic arguments often run along the following lines. Have you made it? Are you a success? Are you prosperous? Have you achieved your ambitions in life? If not, it is because you have failed to trust God. A lack of prosperity means a lack of faith. If you had a real faith in God, he would reward you with health and wealth. Possessions and status are marks of divine favour and human faith. This form of spirituality has had a deep impact upon certain sections of the Christian church. It needs to be challenged – and Luther provides us with a vital resource for doing so.

The implication that wealth and health indicate God's favour is contradicted by Luther, who suggests that suffering is the most authentic token of such favour. To be an authentic Christian is to pass under the shadow of the cross, not to avoid that shadow. For Luther, the 'health and wealth gospel' simply represents an insidious influence of secular standards within Christianity. It is a theology of glory, which knows nothing of the theology of the cross. As Luther once wrote, 'the sign of the Son of man is missing'. A theologian of the cross would insist that the sign of a true and living faith in God is the conformity of the believer to the cross of Jesus Christ – with all its suffering and shame. To be a Christian is to suffer with Christ. Real faith is about being united to Christ, and sharing all that he has to offer – with glory only coming about through the shame, suffering and agony of the cross. There is a strong case to be made for challenging the Christian credentials of those worldly and material philosophies of life, which imply that failure or suffering are a mark of divine rejection. The cross contradicts these outlooks, and suggests that those who promote them are merely substituting secular notions of success and acceptability for their authentically Christian counterparts.

Third, Luther's approach is important in dealing with a group of problems which arise from the excessively experience-orientated attitudes of many Christians. Especially during the first years of faith, many young Christians rely heavily on their experiences of God. Just as the Israelites had the fire and cloudy pillar to reassure them of God's presence and power during their exodus from Egypt, so experience of God is deeply reassuring to many such Christians as they begin their journey into life.

However, a problem usually develops. People often cease experiencing a sense of the presence of God. The fire and cloudy pillar are left behind, as the journey into the wilderness proceeds. Occasionally, this plunges individuals into a state of despair. They do not experience God as present in their lives – and hence they draw the obvious conclusion that God is not present in their lives. Either they have lost their faith, or the entire exercise was a pathetic delusion, from beginning to end.

The theology of the cross mounts a powerful challenge to this excessive reliance upon experience. As we have seen, one of Luther's primary concerns is to stress that the way things are *experienced* often has little bearing on the way things really are. Reflection upon the first Good Friday is enormously helpful in such situations, in that it shows up the serious limitations on the part of experience to discern the presence and activity of God in situations. Luther's fundamental advice to people in such situations remains valid and helpful: stop looking inward, and turn outward to the promises of God. We shall return to this point in the chapter which follows.

Conclusion

So what can we say about the cross, if Luther is right? Perhaps I could end with the following reflections about the cross, bringing together some of Luther's many insights. The cross puts everything to the test. It was from here that the Christian church began its mission – and it is to here that the Christian church must return to rediscover, reclaim, and regain that mission, in order that she may go forward conquering and to conquer in the sign of strength made perfect in weakness: the cross of Jesus Christ.

The legacy of the dying Christ to his disciples and his church was the cross, the symbol of shame, dereliction and despair turned into astonishment and joy by the resurrection from the dead. The cross was no moral victory which vindicated the integrity of the one who died upon it. Without the resurrection, Christianity has nothing to offer the world but some interesting and ultimately sterile ideas. The reason that these ideas did not find their way into the footnotes of some learned work on first-century Jewish sects was the simple and disconcerting fact that the early Christians knew that their Lord and Saviour had been raised from the dead. It was not just that his ideas were vindicated, but that he himself had been raised to glory, propelling his church into the unknown future armed with the knowledge of his continuing redeeming presence (Matthew 28:20). The great Christian themes of hope and joy converge upon the cross of the one who was crucified and raised from the dead. It is through faith in the God who raised Jesus Christ from the dead, who overturned the verdict of the world, that the Christian church must go forward into history, if she is to remain a significant part of that history.

Like a beacon upon a hill, the cross stands as a sign of the love and compassion of God, summoning to its feet sinful humanity. The Christian church is the community which gathers at the foot of that cross to wonder and adore the God who is hidden and yet revealed in its shame and suffering, and who makes so powerful and telling an appeal in his powerlessness and weakness. It is here that the true knowledge of God and ourselves is to be had

– and that knowledge is deeply wounding to both the believer and the church, in that it exposes both for what they really are: naked, weak, impotent, sinful and foolish. Yet it is through being wounded that we are healed, and go forth to heal. It is through recognising our nakedness, weakness, impotence, sinfulness and foolishness that we turn to the God who called the church into being, in order to receive from him healing and wholeness (Revelation 3:17–19), and to offer this healing to others.

The theology of the cross is thus a theology of hope – hope for those who are oppressed by the fear of death, by the seeming meaninglessness of suffering, by the contradictions of Christian experience, by the threat of extinction, by the apparent weakness and foolishness of the Christian gospel. In the tension, the dialectic, between the crucifixion and resurrection lies the key to the Christian understanding of existence, and the recovery of the identity and relevance of the Christian faith and the Christian church. It is a theology of hope for those who despair of the present state of the Christian churches, who wonder how on earth they can even survive, let alone develop. Yet it is not upon human strength and wisdom that the continued existence of the church depends. The graveyards of the world are full of individuals who believed that the existence and life of the church depended upon them, yet the grave could not hold the one upon whom that existence and life ultimately depend. For the theology of the cross involves the recognition that it is *God's* gospel, revealed and made perfect in what the world regarded as stupidity and weakness. The proclamation of the word of the cross has a power of its own, which transcends the weakness and sinfulness of those who proclaim it. The same God who was hidden in the sufferings of the cross is hidden in the weakness of his church, overcoming it and transforming it.

It will, however, be obvious that Luther's theology of the cross has much to say to those who are troubled by doubt and anxiety. This naturally brings us to consider what resources the Reformation makes available to those in such a situation.

5   The Strong Hold of God: Faith, Doubt and Anxiety

Doubt, uncertainty and anxiety possess the potential to paralyse faith. They have the ability to cripple faith, and render it useless as a force for change and good in the world. A spirituality which fails to address and deal with such themes has strictly limited value as a resource for the Christian church. It might therefore seem at first that Reformation spirituality has limited relevance to our modern needs. After all, the sixteenth century is often portrayed as an age of certainties, a period of faith and confidence. For this reason, it is suggested, it is very difficult for modern Christians to have any sense of empathy with this earlier period. The modern era is plagued by doubt, self-questioning and apprehension. How can spirituality of the Reformation, which knew nothing of these radical anxieties, contribute anything to the needs of modern Christians?

This is an important objection, and it needs to be dealt with fully. It is certainly true that uncertainty concerning the future is one of the most noticeable features of modern human existence. In the 1960s, there was considerable anxiety that the human race might destroy itself through a nuclear war. This fear has, for the moment, subsided, only to be replaced by a new series of anxieties: that the human race will destroy planet earth through pollution, or itself through the unchecked spread of AIDS. In addition to this, there is the perennial danger of economic recession, leading to mass unemployment and the

90

collapse of old and familiar patterns of work. The security of traditional ways of life seems constantly under threat from new technology, changing attitudes towards the nuclear family, and the increasing availability and indiscriminate use of narcotics. Tom Wolfe's novel *The Bonfire of the Vanities* captures perfectly this sense of cultural unease among New Yorkers in the late 1980s, viewed through the prism of the events surrounding and following a hit-and-run accident in the city. It is thus relatively easy to regard the past as an era of security. 'They had it so easy!' we think. 'It was easy for them to have faith – they had nothing to worry about.'

In fact, the reason that the past seems so secure to us is that we have the benefit of hindsight. We know that the Cuban missile crisis did not end in a nuclear holocaust; at the time, however, this was far from clear. We know that the build-up of Warsaw Pact military forces during the 1960s and 1970s did not lead to the invasion of western Europe – but many Europeans lived through those years in the fear that precisely this would happen. In fact, just about every period in history is charac- terised by enormous uncertainty concerning the future. The Reformation was no exception. Looking back at it, we think of it as a period of faith; in actuality, it was a period of deep-seated anxiety. Far from being a time of certainty, the Reformation was characterised by serious doubts, scepticism and anxiety about the frailty of human life and the unknown future.

We are now coming to understand why the early sixteenth century was a period of such uncertainty. It may be helpful to identify some of the factors involved. Consider the political arena. Here the order of things seemed totally unstable, poised for radical and unpredictable change. There were strong and persuasive parallels with the collapse of the Roman Empire, which had had such a deep impact upon the thoughts of theo- logians as diverse as Augustine and Pelagius. The old and familiar boundaries, for so long the markers of a stable world, seemed to totter on the brink of collapse. The very existence of Christian Europe could no longer be taken for granted. In 1453, Constantinople finally fell. The last bastion of Christian Europe against the Muslim east had collapsed. The way seemed clear for an inevitable and irreversible expansion of Islam into Europe. By the 1520s, the worst fears of many Europeans seemed adequately justified: the Turks stood at the gates of Vienna.

This external threat was compounded by a new instability within Europe itself. Niccolò Machiavelli typifies the deep sense of unease occasioned by events such as the Franco–Italian war, which seemed to disrupt the security of Renaissance culture. The profound feeling of cultural anxiety and alienation which permeates his correspondence reflects growing disquiet over the way in which brute force seemed capable of disrupting the continuity with the past. The future seemed unknown and unknowable, unpredictable on the basis of past experience. It seemed as if the cultural forces which had given a degree of predictability and constancy to history had been snapped by the higher force of military power. Was this the shape of the future? If so, it seemed unbearable.

Other cohesive social forces were also in the process of dis-integration. The old patrician families, for so long the backbone of society, found themselves being challenged by the mercantile and artisan classes. The shift of power from the former to the latter, especially evident in the imperial cities, seemed to mark the end of an era. In 1499, the power of the patricians in Zurich was finally broken; in Geneva, it survived until 1535, at which point it was finally swept away in the revolution of that year. The stabilising force of tradition, so closely linked with the vested interests of the ancient families, was eroded in the wake of their slide from power.

The church, for so long the bastion and guarantor of social stability, was under threat. As the Reformation gained mo-mentum, the Catholic church, for so long a unifying force in the region, seemed to sway on the brink of degeneration into a loose amalgamation of national churches, each with their own agendas and concerns. The nationalisation of the French church under the Concordat of Bologna (1517) exemplified this trend, as would events in England a decade and a half later. Under the direction of the covetous Henry VIII, the English church lost its long-established and stabilising link with Rome, and began to pursue its own agenda. Further, the threat of national wars –

always a perennial feature of European life – gained credibility
in the period, only to be supplemented by a new menace: the
war of religion. The spread of Protestantism brought in its wake
the danger of a Europe-wide conflict. The scene seemed set
for a struggle of unprecedented scope and intensity. A sense
of nervousness, similar to that evident in English political life on
the eve of the Second World War, pervaded the atmosphere of
the mid-sixteenth century.

Along with this tangible threat to the established order of
society, and perhaps linked to it, came a new development in
political theory. The medieval period had been characterised
by the idea that the social structure was something permanent
and God-given. It was as if the order of things was ordained
by God himself, who hence guaranteed its permanence and
equilibrium. The sixteenth century, however, saw the birth
of a new and radical idea, held by many theorists to lie at the
heart of modern political thought: social order is not something
natural and God-given, but something which is brought into
being and subject to change. The political actuality of change
was thus complemented by a growing theoretical realisation
of the inevitability of change. A sense of unease, of standing
blindfolded on the brink of a crumbling precipice, thus resonates
throughout much of the sacred and secular writings of the early
sixteenth century.

This sense of unease was perhaps most evident in the imperial
cities of Europe, which functioned as observatories from which
their inhabitants could view the changing fabric of European
society around them. Situated at the cultural and economic
crossroads of Europe, the cities were alert to the great political
and social developments taking place around them. Indeed, they
had contributed to their development; it was mainly within the
cities that the stabilising, if stifling, authority of the ancient
patrician families was broken. A deep sense of anxiety, of
uncertainty, resonates throughout those cities at the time. It
is here that a sense of social degeneration, verging on collapse,
is most evident, lent added weight by the shocking effect of
disease upon highly concentrated urban populations. It is es-
timated that at least a quarter, and possibly a third, of the

population of Zurich died from the plague which struck that city in 1519.

Calvin was an especially sensitive observer of such developments, especially within his native France. The situation seemed to be irreversibly locked into decay and decline. There was, he gloomily reflected, a collapse of the social order throughout Europe. Children no longer regarded their parents with any respect. Rulers treated their people with contempt. Wars were longer and more brutal. The magistrates had little concern for justice. Sexual offences were on the increase – rape, incest, adultery and seduction. Religious knowledge had reached an all-time low, with far too many people having only the most rudimentary notion of the gospel. Atheism was growing in importance, especially among the educated and professional classes. Calvin was far more worried about the growth of atheism than the dogged persistence of Roman Catholicism; at least the latter was Christian. Yet even many of the bishops of the church had lost their way, having capitulated to secular ways of thinking, declaring that 'there is no God . . . that everything written and taught about Christ is incorrect and misleading . . . that the doctrines of a life to come and of a final resurrection are mere myths.'

Calvin declared that he had 'been born in a most unhappy age'. It groaned under the weight of calamities and distress. The same circumstances which accompanied the collapse of the Roman Empire, he suggested, had been everywhere apparent during the last thirty or forty years. There is a sense, by no means confined to Calvin, of living in a peculiarly endangered time. It was a low point in human civilisation. What hope could there be? What was there to cling on to in so dark a period? How could one cling on to God at such a time? Indeed, there was a fundamental anxiety, discernible at many levels in society, as to whether there was a God in the first place. The future of Christianity itself seemed open to question – and not merely on account of the Islamic invasion of eastern Europe. The European church seemed incapable of coping with the many threats it faced from within. Perhaps Christianity would not survive the century? The future seemed to lie entirely in the unknown providence of God.

This list could be extended considerably. But the basic point is clear. Reformation spirituality addressed a church which was plagued by anxiety concerning its own future, and that of civilisation in general – anxieties which resonate deeply with the concerns and fears of many modern Christians, making Reformation spirituality not merely a viable, but a valuable, resource for the modern church.

In this atmosphere of uncertainty, it is entirely to be expected that the leading writers of the Reformation should deal with the problem of doubt. This is true even in the case of Calvin, often thought to be the most confident of all the reformers in relation to matters of faith. His definition of faith certainly seems to point in this direction:

> Now we shall have a right definition of faith if we say that it is a steady and certain knowledge of the divine benevolence towards us, which is founded upon the truth of the gracious promise of God in Christ, and is both revealed to our minds and sealed in our hearts by the Holy Spirit.

Yet the *theological* certainty of this statement does not, according to Calvin, necessarily lead to *psychological* security. It is perfectly consistent with a sustained wrestling with doubt and anxiety on the part of the believer.

> When we stress that faith ought to be certain and secure, we do not have in mind a certainty without doubt, or a security without any anxiety. Rather, we affirm that believers have a perpetual struggle with their own lack of faith, and are far from possessing a peaceful conscience, never interrupted by any disturbance. On the other hand, we want to deny that they may fall out of, or depart from, their confidence in the divine mercy, no matter how much they may be troubled.

The importance of this passage is confirmed by his comments on Mark 9:24 – 'Lord, I believe; help thou my unbelief':

> He declares that he believes, and yet confesses his unbelief. Although these two things seem inconsistent, in fact there is

no one who does not experience much the same thing inwardly. A perfect faith is nowhere to be found, so it follows that all of us are partly unbelievers. Yet in his kindness, God pardons us and reckons us to be believers upon account of our small portion of faith. For our part, we ought to try to get rid of the unbelief that remains within us, and fight against it and ask the Lord to correct it. And as often as we struggle, we must flee to him for comfort. If we consider carefully what God has given each of us, it will become very clear that hardly anyone has a strong faith, a few have a middling sort of faith, and most of us have only a small measure of faith.

Perhaps Calvin is hinting that he himself has only a 'small measure of faith'? But his point is clear: the life of faith is a severe struggle for most of us. Commenting on Calvin's doctrine of faith, Edward A. Dowey writes:

If the bare words of his definition of faith make it 'steady and certain knowledge', according to Calvin, we must notice that such faith never is realised. We could formulate a description of existing faith for him as 'a steady and certain knowledge invariably attacked by vicious doubts and fears over which it is finally victorious'.

Faith is sustained by hope – a confident expectation that the contradictions and disappointments of this world will be resolved and ended from the perspective of the resurrection. As Calvin stated this point in the *Genevan Catechism*:

Faith believes that God is real; hope awaits for the moment when he will demonstrate his reality. Faith believes that God is our father; hope believes that he will always behave as a father towards us. Faith believes that we have been given eternal life; hope awaits the day when it will be revealed. Faith is the foundation upon which hope rests; hope nourishes and shelters faith.

So how did Reformation spirituality address the problem of doubt and anxiety? What resources was it able to deploy within this atmosphere of uncertainty? To begin our discussion of this question, we may consider the Reformation understanding of the nature of faith itself.

The Nature of Faith

The most significant contribution to the classic Evangelical understanding of faith was unquestionably made by Martin Luther. Luther's doctrine of justification by faith alone (see chapter 9) made faith, rightly understood, the cornerstone of his spirituality and theology. Luther's fundamental point is that 'the Fall' (Genesis 1–3) is first and foremost a *fall from faith*. Faith is the right relationship with God (cf. Genesis 15:6). To have faith is to live as God intends us to live.

Three points relating to Luther's idea of faith may be singled out as having special importance to Reformation spirituality. Each of these points is taken up and developed by later writers, such as Calvin, indicating that Luther has made a fundamental contribution to the development of Reformation thought at this point. These three points are:

1. Faith has a personal, rather than a purely historical, reference.
2. Faith concerns trust in the promises of God.
3. Faith unites the believer to Christ.

We shall consider each of these points individually.

First, faith is not simply historical knowledge. Luther argues that a faith which is content to believe in the historical reliability of the gospels is not a saving faith. Sinners are perfectly capable of trusting in the historical details of the gospels; but these facts of themselves are not adequate for true Christian faith. Saving faith concerns believing and trusting that Christ was born *pro nobis*, born for us personally, and has accomplished for us the work of salvation. As Luther puts this point:

I have often spoken about two different kinds of faith. The first goes like this: you believe that it is true that Christ is the person who is described and proclaimed in the gospels, but you do not believe that he is such a person for you. You doubt if you can receive that from him, and you think: 'Yes, I'm sure he is that person for someone else (like Peter and Paul, and for religious and holy people). But is he that person for me? Can I confidently expect to receive everything from him that the saints expect?' You see, this faith is nothing. It receives nothing of Christ, and tastes nothing of him either. It cannot feel joy, nor love of him or for him. This is a faith related to Christ, but not a faith in Christ . . . The only faith which deserves to be called Christian is this: you believe unreservedly that it is not only for Peter and the saints that Christ is such a person, but also for you yourself – in fact, for you more than anyone else.

The second point concerns faith as 'trust' (*fiducia*). The notion of trust is prominent in the Reformation conception of faith, as a nautical analogy used by Luther indicates: 'Everything depends upon faith. The person who does not have faith is like someone who has to cross the sea, but is so frightened that he does not trust the ship. And so he stays where he is, and is never saved, because he will not get on board and cross over.' Faith is not merely believing that something is true; it is being prepared to act upon that belief, and relying upon it. To use Luther's analogy: faith is not simply about believing that a ship exists – it is about stepping into it, and entrusting ourselves to it.

But what are we being asked to trust? Are we being asked simply to have faith in faith? The question could perhaps be phrased more accurately: *Whom* are we being asked to trust? For Luther, the answer was unequivocal: faith is about being prepared to put one's trust in the promises of God, and the integrity and faithfulness of the God who made those promises.

It is necessary that the man who is about to confess his sins put his trust only and completely in the most gracious promise of God. That is, he must be certain that the one who has promised forgiveness to the man who confesses his sins will most faithfully fulfil his promise. For we are to glory, not in the fact that we confess our sins, but in the fact that God has promised pardon to those who confess their sins. In other words, we are not to glory on account of the worthiness or adequacy of our confession (because there is no such worthiness or adequacy) but on account of the truth and certainty of his promises.

Faith is only as strong as the one in whom we believe and trust. The efficacy of faith does not rest upon the intensity with which we believe, but in the reliability of the one in whom we believe. It is not the greatness of our faith, but the greatness of God, which counts. As Luther put it:

> Even if my faith is weak, I still have exactly the same treasure and the same Christ as others. There is no difference . . . It is like two people, each of whom owns a hundred guldens. One may carry them around in a paper sack, the other in an iron chest. But despite these differences, they both own the same treasure. Thus the Christ who you and I own is one and the same, irrespective of the strength or weakness of your faith or mine.

The content of faith matters at least as much as, and probably far more than, its intensity. It is pointless to trust passionately in someone who is not worthy of trust; even a modicum of faith in someone who is totally reliable is vastly to be preferred. Trust is not, however, an occasional attitude. For Luther, it is an undeviating trusting outlook upon life, a constant stance of conviction of the trustworthiness of the promises of God.

This analysis brings out a point of fundamental importance for Christian spirituality. Faith is not merely, nor even primarily, an act of understanding. It is an act of will. It is a decision to trust in the person and promises of God, despite the intellectual doubts and difficulties which may arise. It is a deliberate decision to commit oneself to God. The will to believe thus often comes into conflict with disconfirming evidence, which suggests that this decision, this act of will, was ill-informed. A potential struggle between the intellect and the will is the direct outcome of this understanding of the nature of faith. In that the intellect draws heavily upon reason and experience in shaping its judgements, it is thus inevitable that Reformation spirituality is obliged to address the question of the *reliability* of reason and experience as theological resources. Luther's theology of the cross, as we have seen (pp. 69–85) is an excellent case in point.

The third point is that faith unites the believer to Christ. This point is of such importance to Christian spirituality that we may consider it in some depth. In what way does the believer relate to Jesus Christ? The history of Christian spirituality presents us with two main options. In the first place, the believer is understood to relate to Christ in an external manner. Christ is the example of the Christian life, which the believer is required to imitate. The theme of the 'imitation of Christ' (*imitatio Christi*) is of especial importance to the writers of the spiritual revival known as the *Devotio Moderna*, such as Thomas à Kempis. The believer is required to imitate the example of Christ, 'whom the Father sent into the world as an example of all virtues', by self-mortification, humility, self-renunciation and a contempt for the world. 'Whoever wishes to understand and rejoice in the words of Christ must endeavour to conform his whole life to him.' Johann von Staupitz, Luther's superior within the Augustinian Order, also echoes this idea.

> Christ is a model given by God, according to which I would work, suffer and die. He is the only model which anyone can follow in which everything that is good in life, suffering and death is usefully set out. Therefore nobody can act, suffer or die correctly, unless it happens in conformity with the life, suffering and death of Christ.

This idea gained new influence in the early sixteenth century, not least through the influence of Erasmus of Rotterdam. Erasmus had been influenced by the Brethren of the Common Life, the monastic movement especially linked with the *Devotio Moderna*, who had a particular following in his native Low Countries. Erasmus uses the phrase 'philosophy of Christ' (*philosophia Christi*) to refer to the conformity of the believer to the example of Christ. The gospel, according to Erasmus, is primarily *lex Christi*, 'the law of Christ' – in other words, something which is to be obeyed. Reformers sympathetic to Erasmus, such as Martin Bucer, developed a spirituality in which the believer is aided by the Holy Spirit to conform to the example of Christ, and thus fulfil the new law which he came to establish.

If this is one way of exploring the relation of the believer and Christ, it was one which was rejected by most of the reformers. One of the most characteristic features of Reformation spirituality is its insistence upon a transformative encounter between the believer and the risen Christ, brought about through faith. This encounter is conceived in strongly personal terms. Christ is not set outside us and at a distance, but rather comes to dwell within us, transforming us from within.

Luther states this principle clearly in his 1520 writing, *The Liberty of a Christian.*

> Faith unites the soul with Christ as a bride is united with her bridegroom. As Paul teaches us, Christ and the soul become one flesh by this mystery (Ephesians 5:31–2). And if they are one flesh, and if the marriage is for real – indeed, it is the most perfect of all marriages, and human marriages are poor examples of this one true marriage – then it follows that everything that they have is held in common, whether good or evil. So the believer can boast of and glory of whatever Christ possesses, as though it were his or her own; and whatever the believer has, Christ claims as his own. Let us see how this works out, and see how it benefits us. Christ is full of grace, life and salvation. The human soul is full of sin, death and damnation. Now let faith come between them. Sin, death and damnation will be Christ's. And grace, life and salvation will be the believer's.

Faith, then, is not assent to an abstract set of doctrines. Rather, it is a 'wedding ring' (Luther), pointing to mutual commitment and union between Christ and the believer. It is the response of the whole person of the believer to God, which leads in turn to the real and personal presence of Christ in the believer. 'To know Christ is to know his benefits,' wrote Philip Melanchthon, Luther's colleague at Wittenberg. Faith makes both Christ and his benefits – such as forgiveness, justification and hope – available to the believer. Calvin makes this point with characteristic clarity: 'Having ingrafted us into his body, [Christ] makes us partakers, not only of all his benefits, but also of himself.' Christ, Calvin insists, is not 'received merely in the understanding and imagination. For the promises offer him, not so that we end up with the mere sight and knowledge of him, but that we enjoy a true communication of him.'

Having discussed the nature of faith, we are now in a position to begin considering the problem of doubt.

Wrestling with Doubt and Uncertainty

Time and time again, the reformers stress one simple point: it is perfectly possible to be a Christian, and at the same time to be troubled by doubt. Doubt is not a symptom of unbelief. Faith, like unbelief, is an act of will. Faith is a deliberate decision to live *as if* Christianity is true, in the firm and confident expectation that it will one day be shown beyond all doubt that Christianity *is* true. While documenting the Reformation emphasis upon faith as trust (*fiducia*), I made the point that this approach inevitably entailed a tension between the will and the intellect. In that the intellect relied upon reason and experience in drawing its conclusions, the scene is set for a potential conflict between the will and the intellect; between faith on the one hand, and reason and experience on the other.

Reformation spirituality developed two main strategies for coping with this sort of doubt and anxiety. In the first place, the reliability of reason and experience were called into question. If reason or experience seemed to contradict the promises of God, why should we be tempted to believe that they were somehow more reliable than those promises? In the second place, the weakness of human faith, considered as an act of will, was stressed. Doubt is a symptom of a lack of will on our part to place our trust fully in the promises of God. The first approach is especially associated with Luther, the second with Calvin. We shall consider them individually.

Perhaps the central anxiety which Reformation spirituality addresses is the tension between faith and experience – a tension which perplexes and bewilders many today. How can I have any degree of certainty or hope, in the face of the fact that I experience so many things in life which challenge my faith. Faith and experience exist in an unresolved tension, which threatens to collapse under pressure. A central question of Christian spirituality, given new urgency at the time of the Reformation, concerns how these potentially opposing forces may be held in a stable equilibrium. Perhaps I could use the phrase 'the fragility of faith' to indicate the problem at issue here.

Perhaps the most powerful and insightful discussion of this spiritually important theme is found in the early writings of Martin Luther. 'Faith', wrote Luther, 'is a free surrender and a joyful wager on the unseen, untried and unknown goodness of God.' This remarkable definition of faith contains at its core, not the idea of total certainty of conviction, but the element of both the unknown and the unknowable. There are strong anticipations here of a Kierkegaardian leap of faith. To become a Christian – indeed, to *be* a Christian – is to plunge into darkness and doubt. It is to detach oneself from the security and certainty of the visible and tangible world. 'To believe in Christ is the most difficult of all things, in that it is to be moved from the world of the senses – interior and exterior – into the world which lies beyond the senses, namely into the invisible, most high and incomprehensible God.' Already, we can discern one of the hallmarks of Luther's characteristic notion of faith – its break with the world of human experience.

In a remarkable sermon of 30 November 1516, Luther develops an illustration which highlights this tension between faith and the world of the senses and experience. Christ was raised up from the earth upon the cross, denied any foothold upon the ground. And in the same way, Luther suggests, faith is, so to speak, suspended in mid-air, with no grounding in experience. To believe in Christ is to turn away from the world of experience, and to put one's trust in the invisible and intangible promises of God. 'Faith unites the soul with the invisible, unutterable, eternal and unthinkable word of God, while at the same time it separates it from all things visible and tangible.' Faith thus exists in tension with experience and reason, which continually seek to anchor the believer firmly to the everyday world. Faith aims to break this oppressive bond to the mundane and restrictive world of human thought and experience, in order to allow the individual to encounter the living God.

Luther uses the image of darkness to capture this ambiguity of faith. Faith is permanently, so to speak, partly in the dark about the purposes and strategies of God. 'We have all been taught that we ought to hope for divine assistance in times of temptation. But the time, manner and nature of that assistance are unknown to us . . . Thus the eye of faith looks towards the deep darkness and blackness of the hill – and sees nothing.' Faith and doubt, like righteousness and sin, co-exist in the believer (see pp. 157–61). Just as the Christian is at one and the same time righteous and sinful (*simul iustus et peccator*), so he or she is also at one and the same time a believer and a doubter. The promises of God evoke and confirm faith; our experience of the world disconfirms this faith, and evokes doubt.

Luther's language and imagery clearly point to the cross of Christ as the supreme paradigm of the situation of the believer. Indeed, Luther's understanding of the relation of faith and doubt is part and parcel of his 'theology of the cross'. The cross represents the focus of God's self-revelation. It is here that God has decided to make himself known to us. But as experience contemplates Calvary, it rapidly comes to the conclusion that God is conspicuously absent from that scene. It is a scene of apparent hopelessness and helplessness. It is a scene of desertion, dereliction and death. There is no sign whatsoever of the presence and power of God. The only obvious outcome of Calvary is doubt and scepticism concerning the existence, nature and power of the God who is alleged to be implicated.

That preliminary judgement of experience is overturned and discredited through the resurrection. The promise of vindication and resurrection was there, but ignored. By trusting in experience, rather than the promises of God, those around the cross found themselves thrown into a situation of doubt and despair. The resurrection of Christ demonstrated God's fidelity to his promises. For Luther, the cross represents an object lesson in faith: look outside yourself to the promises of God, rather than inside yourself to your feelings and experiences. It is the former which evoke and sustain faith; the latter merely confuse and weaken it. 'Faith is nothing else than the adherence to the word of God.' The cross of Christ illuminates our own situation of doubt.

> For it is a difficult thing – indeed, it is the power of divine grace – to believe in God as the one who lifts up our head and crowns us in the midst of death and hell. For this exaltation is a hidden affair. What we actually see is only despair. There is no help from God. And so we are taught to believe in hope against hope. The wisdom of the cross is today deeply hidden in a profound mystery. For there is no other way into heaven than through this cross of Christ.

The idea being developed here is that God has entered into this world of darkness, confusion and mystery. He has chosen to reveal himself in an historical event which brings together at a single focus the central anxieties of human existence – the dreadful sense of meaninglessness and emptiness of life, the fear of suffering and death, and the sickening feeling that God is not there. Far from avoiding these enigmas, uncertainties and riddles, God chooses to engage directly with them.

The theme here is that of defeating death and doubt with their own weapons. This idea is expressed especially well in Nicolas Cabasilas' *On Life in Christ*:

> As we were cut off from God in three ways – by our nature, by our sins, and by our death – the Saviour worked in such a way that we could meet him unobstructed, and come to be with him directly. This he did by removing these obstacles, one by one. He removed the first by sharing in our human nature, and the second by going through the death of the cross. The third wall of division was removed when he rose from the dead, and banished the tyranny of death from our nature.

God chose to fight these enemies of faith on their own territory and on their own terms. For Luther, doubt and anxiety are to be added to these hostile forces. God redeemed us, not merely from sin, but from its ally, doubt. And just as sin continues to have a hold upon us after we have been justified, so doubt continues to be a feature of the Christian life. The believer is simultaneously a believer and a doubter. The struggle against doubt, like the battle against sin, is a perennial feature of the Christian life.

The Christian, according to Luther, may expect to continue to be troubled by doubt and anxiety. They, like sin and evil, will continue to assault believers throughout their lives of faith. Nevertheless, Luther insists, their bluff has been called. The victory of the cross includes the showing up of doubt for what it really is – an inability to discern the hidden presence of God in his world, or an unwillingness to allow that the hand of God is at work in situations from which he appears to be absent.

For Luther, Christianity ultimately stands or falls with the trustworthiness and reliability of the God who raised Jesus Christ from the dead. By meditating on that first Good Friday, we can remind ourselves of the unreliability of our own judgement on the one hand, and the faithfulness of God to his promises on the other – and thus we can put doubt in its proper perspective. For, seen properly, doubt is not a threat to faith, but a reminder of how fragile a hold we have on our knowledge of God, and how gracious God is in having revealed himself to us. For, without God's revelation of himself, we would have been left totally in the dark concerning him and his love for us. God is not capricious or whimsical, nor does he fail to stand by his promises or to act in accordance with his nature and character, as we know it through Scripture and through Jesus Christ. Instead, we know a God who is faithful to his covenant, who promises mercy and forgiveness to those who put their trust in him. Instead of trusting in our own perception of a situation, or relying upon our feelings and emotions, we should learn to trust in the faithfulness and constancy of God.

The second approach to doubt is found in the writings of John Calvin. Faith is an act of will, which presupposes a struggle of the will. In an earlier chapter, we noted Calvin's characteristic emphasis upon the inter-relatedness of our knowledge of God and our knowledge of ourselves; the two cannot be had in isolation. It is one thing to know God as the totally reliable and unfailing creator and sustainer of the world, and as the one who promises us salvation through Christ – but that knowledge cannot be had in isolation from knowledge of ourselves as fallen, frail and sinful.

The point that Calvin is making is the following. Faith is indeed 'a steady and certain knowledge of the divine benevolence towards us, which is founded upon the truth of the gracious promise of God in Christ' – but this is to deal only with the God-ward side of the definition. What of the other partner to this knowledge – ourselves? Knowledge of God goes hand in hand with knowledge of ourselves. And what do we know about ourselves? That sin prevents us from willing to trust God fully. Calvin's understanding of the nature of faith, linked with his insistence upon the inseparability of the knowledge of God and of ourselves, thus provides a framework for making sense of doubt.

> When I stress that faith ought to be certain and secure, I do not mean a certainty without doubt, or a security troubled by no anxiety. Rather, I am saying that believers have a perpetual conflict with their own lack of trust. They are far from having peaceful consciences, never bothered by any disturbance. Yet on the other hand, I deny that believers – no matter how much they may be troubled – may ever fall from that certain trust which they have put in the divine mercy.

Calvin thus suggests that doubt and anxiety are essentially due to a lack of trust in God. This reflects a shortcoming on our part, rather than upon the part of God. Unbelief must be recognised as a constituent element of faith (although Calvin will not lend it dignity by including reference to it in his definition of faith). 'In the present life, we are never so fortunate as to be cured of the disease of mistrust, and entirely filled and possessed by faith. And so conflicts arise, when unbelief, which remains in what is left of our former natures, rises up to attack faith.' We are never entirely faith-full, according to Calvin; and therein lies the root of doubt.

For Calvin, therefore, one method of coping with doubt is to renew our commitment to God in a revitalised act of will. 'Here is the main hinge upon which faith turns: that we do not regard the promises of mercy which God offers to us as true only outside ourselves, but not at all within us. Rather, we should make them ours by inwardly embracing them. And so at last the confidence which Paul somewhere calls "peace" is born.' Calvin develops the theme of the life of faith as a struggle against doubt – yet a struggle which can be won, and which can deepen the quality of faith through engagement with doubt. Faith grows through being put to the test.

Calvin's basic point here could be rephrased along the following lines. Doubt is not so much a matter of the head; it is a matter of the heart. Doubt is not simply about intellectual difficulties or hesitations concerning the gospel; it concerns a radical lack of willingness on the part of the sinful human heart to trust fully in the goodness of God. The root of doubt is to be sought in the ambiguities and equivocations of our emotions, as much as in the mental riddles and enigmas which confront our minds. Earlier, we noted Luther's analogy of faith and a boat (p. 98). We could say that Calvin's point is that doubt is not simply hesitation about whether that boat exists or not; it is a hesitation about whether to get into it or not. We are reluctant to commit ourselves to that boat, as we are fearful about the possible consequences. For Calvin, a realistic strategy for coping with doubt involves commitment: one must set one's hesitations to one side, get in, and set off. One must, to use a slightly different analogy, burn one's bridges, to prevent a retreat arising from a weakness of will or a lack of heart.

Furthermore, Calvin suggests, the Psalms bear witness to similar struggles with doubt on the part of believers. In an aside, Calvin made the comment that his own personal difficulties and doubts were of considerable assistance to him when reading the Psalter; they enabled him to gain a deeper sense of the meanings of texts, which otherwise might have been difficult to expound. For example, when commenting on Psalm 22:1 ('My God, my God, why have you forsaken me?'), Calvin writes as follows:

This is precisely what all believers experience daily . . . When someone is overwhelmed by this kind of perplexity, it submerges them in unbelief, and they are no longer willing to do anything about it. But if faith should come to their aid, in opposition to this, the same person who, on the basis of the evidence, regarded God as cross or alienated discovers his hidden and secret grace in the mirror of the promises. They alternate between two contradictory states of mind. On the one hand Satan, showing the signs of the wrath of God, urges them to despair and tries to cause them to fall; on the other, faith recalls them to the promise, teaches them to wait patiently, and to trust in God until he again shows his fatherly face.

Calvin thus argues that doubt is a natural feature of the Christian life, arising from and reflecting continued unbelief within the human heart. But, he argues, this unbelief can be fought, and eventually mastered.

'Faith needs the Word as much as fruit needs the living root of a tree . . . Faith vanishes unless it is supported by the Word.' It is for this reason that Scripture figures so prominently in Calvin's spirituality. For Calvin, Scripture is the food of faith, the life-giving and nourishing foundation of the Christian life. 'Faith is a knowledge of the divine will towards us, received from his Word.' However, Calvin is more precise: it is not the Word of God in general, but the promises of God, which is the specific object of faith. 'We make the foundation of faith the gracious promise . . . Time and time again, Paul treats faith and the gospel as correlatives.' While Calvin is concerned not to imply that certain parts of Scripture are inherently less valuable than others, he nevertheless insists upon the centrality of those witnessing to God's gracious promises: 'When I say that faith must be grounded in the gracious promise, I am not denying that believers embrace and accept the Word of God in all its parts. Rather, I am designating the promise of mercy as its proper object.'

That promise of mercy reaches its climax and fulfilment in Jesus Christ. Calvin here echoes a central theme of the Reformation. Scripture contains the promises of God, confirmed and given substance through Jesus Christ. For Calvin, 'everything which faith ought to contemplate is shown to us in Christ.' Scripture, for Luther, is 'the manger in which Christ is laid'. It is through reflection and meditation upon Scripture that faith

may be nourished and strengthened. It is through being willing
to accept these promises as true that doubt can be held in check.
Calvin advises those who are troubled by doubt to reflect upon
Christ, and draw comfort and assurance by doing so.

> God's adoption of us in Christ is for no other end than that we
> should be considered his children. Now Scripture declares that
> all who believe in the only-begotten Son of God are the children
> and heirs of God . . . Christ is the mirror in which we are called
> upon to view the eternal and hidden election of God. He is the
> surety of that election. And faith is the eye, by which we see the
> eternal life which God presents to us in this mirror. And faith is
> the hand by which we take hold of this surety and pledge.

For Calvin, then, doubt arises not on account of any lack
of trustworthiness on the part of God, nor on the part of his
promises revealed and declared in Scripture. Faith may rest
assured of the total faithfulness, integrity and trustworthiness
of God. Rather, the problem arises within the human will, which
is reluctant to commit itself to those promises. It wants to hold
back. It is in two minds. The problem of doubt rests in our
hesitation and reluctance to commit ourselves totally to God.

Calvin's solution is not a simplistic declaration or demand –
'You must believe harder! You must have more faith!' A weak
faith is a real faith. The English reformer John Rogers put this
point well: 'Weak faith is true faith – as precious, though not
as great as strong faith: the same Holy Spirit the author; the
same gospel the instrument . . . For it is not the strength of
our faith that saves, but the truth of our faith.' Calvin draws
our attention to the weakness of will with which we embrace
the gospel. We need to be gently and tenderly persuaded that
we can wholly trust in God. The resilient bonds which keep us
linked to our unredeemed tendency to trust only what we can
see, hear and touch need to be broken. Calvin suggests that
sanctification includes a growing willingness and ability to allow
a faith of the mind to be transformed into a faith of the heart.
We need to develop a *will* to believe.

We should not have faith in faith itself. That outlook on life
is condemned to be plagued by doubts such as 'I haven't enough

faith,' or 'I just don't trust in Christ enough.' Calvin's point is that you believe, not in the quality of your personal faith, but in the reliability of God. You do not trust in the intensity of your faith, but in the commitment of God to his promises. To have faith in faith is to put your trust in your own ability to believe, rather than in God's ability to save. You are looking inward, contemplating your own mental state, when you should be looking outward, contemplating the promises of God, confirmed by the death and resurrection of Jesus Christ and the sending of the Holy Spirit.

We are not, therefore, being asked to believe harder that God is loving; we are being asked to allow our lives and wills to be shaped by our faith in a loving God. We are not being asked to have more faith in eternal life; we are being asked to allow our faith in eternal life to affect us more deeply here and now. If faith remains something which affects only our minds, it will be prone to doubt and indecision. It must transform our wills and our lives – and, by doing so, the quiet confidence of true Christian faith results. As Calvin put it, 'Faith is not a naked and frigid awareness of Christ, but a living and real experience of his power, which produces confidence.'

A faith which remains purely intellectual is a faith which has yet to discover the power and the peace of God – and doubt is both a symptom of that failure, and a stimulus to discover the new depths of faith and commitment which await us in the gospel. Faith is not merely about believing that God is there – it is about letting oneself fall into the arms of God. Spiritual anxiety is an invitation to enter into a new quality of life, denied to us thus far on account of our inadequate grasp of the God who promises himself to us through Jesus Christ – denied to us, not on account of any inadequacy on the part of God, but through our inadequate perception of and response to him. Real faith allows us to live in the world in peace, through a secure relationship with the one who has created and called us.

The 'assurance of faith' thus rests upon the total trustworthiness of the God who creates and redeems us. The grounds of our assurance lie not in ourselves, but in the promises of God. To reassure ourselves of our faith or our salvation, we are directed to look outside of ourselves, away from our subjective feelings and emotions, and to look instead towards the promises of God, declared in Scripture and sealed by the death and resurrection of Christ.

Reformation spirituality thus has a significant contribution to make to the modern church at this point. Anxiety and doubt continue to be a disturbing and perplexing feature of Christian life. Writers such as Luther and Calvin cast light on how they arise, and have helpful – and, as experience suggests, *viable* – suggestions to make to allow us and our people to cope with them, and even to learn from them. A stable and reliable foundation is thus laid for Christian life in the world. But life in the everyday world raises a cluster of very difficult questions for Christian spirituality – questions which must be addressed, if responsible Christian life in the everyday world is to be a real possibility. How can we get the balance right between God and his world, between the creator and his creation? How can we affirm the world without unintentionally denying God? And what is the value of human work in the everyday world? What purpose does it serve? What is its basic motivation? The next two chapters develop the important resources which Reformation spirituality places at our disposal in this respect. We begin by considering how a responsible Christian attitude towards the world may be developed and sustained.

6   Faith in the City:
A Critical World-affirming
Spirituality

The Christian imagination has always been controlled by certain foundational images. One of the greatest tragedies of Christian spirituality is that the sheer freshness and excitement of many of these images has been lost. We do not know who, in a dazzling moment of inspired insight, first saw guilt as dirt which needed to be washed away. Nor can we be entirely sure when someone for the very first time watched a living spring burst forth from the desert rocks, and saw in this a brilliant analogy of the transformation of human life through the presence of God. Sadly, we have become used to these images. They have become stale, and have lost the freshness of their moment of discovery. One of the central and most urgent tasks of Christian spirituality is to allow these images to be born again – to see them as if for the very first time, savouring their richness and depth. It was C. S. Lewis who taught us to rediscover and value the Christian imagination; it is Christian spirituality which must provide it with the images which it needs for its stimulation.

One of those images is that of a city. Sections of the Old Testament resonate with the praise of the city of Jerusalem, which is seen both as a tangible image of the presence and providence of God amongst his people, and also as a pointer to the fulfilment of messianic expectations. The New Testament gives a new twist to this focus, not least in the remarkable reworking of the theme of the 'city of God' found in the Revelation of

St John. For this biblical writer, the fulfilment of all Christian hopes and expectations centres upon the new Jerusalem, the city of God within which the Lamb reigns. For Augustine of Hippo, the conflict between the 'city of God' and the 'city of the world' underlies the quest for responsible Christian political and social action. The early Puritans, founding settlements in the Massachusetts Bay area, found inspiration in the biblical image of the city on the hill. Boston was to become the American Geneva, the city of God which would draw all comers to its powerful and purifying light.

The theme of the city is of central importance to Reformation spirituality, not least on account of the fact that the Reformation was an urban phenomenon. It was the great imperial cities of Europe which set the pace for adopting the Reformation. Zurich, Strasbourg and Geneva are three examples of the great walled cities of Europe which came to see themselves as bastions of Evangelical truth and fervour, strongholds of faith from which the conversion of the surrounding regions might be undertaken. The iconography which came to surround the city of Geneva illustrates this point well: for many writers of the sixteenth century, Geneva was a citadel of true Christian spirituality, a beacon of light in a hitherto notably dark corner of Europe.

It is of note that, in this sense, Luther is not representative of the reformers as a whole. Where Luther was concerned with reforming an unsophisticated rural region of northern Germany, governed by a prince, and geared largely to a quasi-feudal agrarian economy centring upon the peasant, his colleagues further south and west were confronting a radically different situation. Zwingli in Zurich, Bucer in Strasbourg, Vadian in St Gallen, and Calvin in Geneva (to name but a few) were obliged to work within the sophisticated power structures of modern urban societies, which had chosen to set behind them the feudal ways of the great old families, and embrace new ways of acting and thinking.

Where Luther had to wrestle with the vagaries of the local aristocracy, Calvin was confronted with professional self-made persons, who had won their authority within the city by personal effort. The phenomenon of the self-made person – so central a feature of modern western culture, and posing such fundamental problems for Christian spirituality – has its origins in the imperial cities of the early sixteenth century. The imperial cities of Germany and Switzerland were the crucibles within which many of the distinctive political, social and economic ideas of the modern period were to come to birth. Where Luther's theology took on a distinctively individualist tone, Calvin's was orientated towards the needs of a definite community – the city of Geneva.

The City and the Community of Faith

From what has been said thus far, it will be clear that the image of a city points to a communal, as opposed to a purely individualist, conception of the Christian life. Salvation, like sin, has both individual and corporate dimensions. The church is seen as a body, an institution within which faith may be nourished and sustained. As Calvin stated this point:

> I shall begin then, with the church, into the bosom of which God is pleased to gather his children, not only so that they may be nourished by her assistance and ministry while they are infants and children, but also so that they may be guided by her motherly care until they mature and reach the goal of faith. 'For what God has joined together, no one shall divide' (Mark 10:9). For those to whom God is Father, the church shall also be their mother.

The visible institution of the church is thus treated as a fundamental resource for the life of faith. It is here that believers may encounter and support one another, and find mutual encouragement through praising God and hearing his word. The image of the 'church as mother' (an image which Calvin gladly borrows from Cyprian of Carthage) underscores the corporate dimensions of Christian faith:

> Let us learn from this simple word 'mother' how useful (indeed, how necessary) it is to know her. There is no other way to life, unless this mother conceives us in her womb, nourishes us at her breast, and keeps us under her care and guidance.

Powerful theological imagery nestles within this way of speaking, above all that of the word of God which conceives us within the womb of the church. But it is the practical aspects of this way of thinking about the church which command our attention at this point. The institution of the church is a necessary, helpful, God-given and God-ordained means of spiritual growth and development. It is meant to be there – and it is meant to be used. The Christian is not meant to be, nor called to be, a radical and solitary romantic, wandering in isolated loneliness through the world; rather, the Christian is called to be a member of a community. The image of a city helpfully points to this ineradicable element of responsible and authentic Evangelical spirituality.

It is fair to suggest that contemporary Evangelicalism has often lost sight of this aspect of Reformation spirituality. The Renaissance rediscovery of the individual led to the Reformation placing considerable emphasis upon the need to make faith relevant to the individual – an emphasis which modern Evangelicalism has easily and gladly carried over from its origins in the sixteenth century. Yet this new emphasis upon the personal appropriation of faith was not understood by the reformers to involve a rejection, or even a weakening, of the corporate aspects of faith. The new stress upon the need to appropriate faith personally was firmly set in the context of maintaining an already existing emphasis upon the importance of the community of faith to spiritual growth and development.

Modern Evangelicals can, and must, reclaim this aspect of their heritage. For Calvin, the community of faith was there because it was meant to be there – a God-given and God-ordained means of spiritual discipline and pastoral care. Calvin gladly took up the New Testament emphasis upon the body of Christ, in the knowledge that Evangelicalism was being spread and consolidated by communities of faith throughout the kingdom of France. For Calvin, an emphasis upon the communal aspects of faith remained faithful to the New Testament, made theological sense – and worked in practice. Communities of faith provided vital support groups, which kept faith going and growing, even under the most difficult of circumstances.

The Development of a World-affirming Spirituality

The Reformation took place within some of the most culturally advanced and socially sophisticated centres of Europe. It was no backward-looking phenomenon, which took place in isolated and insignificant backwaters; rather, it took place within some of the most advanced and refined communities of the era. Individuals such as Calvin were thus obliged to face the problems and opportunities of early modern urban life, anticipating many of the difficulties and possibilities to which their successors are heirs. It was neither possible nor desirable for the urban reformers to disengage from their social situation. They were obliged to affirm and to enter fully into the life of the cities – yet to do so in such a way that did not compromise their Christian convictions. Calvin could not reform Geneva solely through the pulpit or the printing press; he had to engage directly with the realities of political power within the city.

This posed serious practical and theoretical difficulties. Calvin had to be alert to the ways of the world, if he was to change the ways of that world. The difficulties which Calvin confronted as he negotiated with the power-brokers of the city are a matter of history, as is his determination to engage with the world, in order to claim that world for its creator. Calvin's theology neatly corresponds to the realities of life at Geneva: you have to deal with the world as it is, in order to make it what you want it to be. In a fallen world, you must expect to get your hands dirty.

To anticipate some of the difficulties which this raised, we may reflect further upon the image of the city. Thus far, we have viewed this image in a positive light; it is now necessary to note that it can also assume a more negative function. It is no accident that Augustine chose to highlight the dialectic between God and the world with his theme of the two cities – the city of God, and the city of the world. The city can also come to stand as a symbol of the forces which threaten to cripple or destroy the life of faith. The early monastic movement in Egypt, centring upon individuals such as Anthony, arose through a conviction that the moral and spiritual atmosphere of the cities of the period was so polluted that faith could not survive; it was necessary to set up a separate community in the desert, isolated and insulated from the influences which caused faith to diminish the world. 'The desert became a city,' wrote Anthony's biographer, capturing both the demographic and spiritually symbolic aspects of this development. A stronghold of faith had been created – the city. But it was a city of faith, opposed to the secular cities which the monks had left.

In our own day, the image of the city has altered considerably, taking on strongly negative associations. When Harvey Cox wrote his influential work *The Secular City*, back in the heyday of the 'no-God' movement of the 1960s, it seemed that the city was the symbol of human autonomy and achievement. The cities of the world seemed vibrant with new life and creativity. London and New York were exciting places to be at the time. They seemed admirably suited to be symbols of the new secular age which Cox believed to be dawning. The great cities of the world were potent icons of a world come of age, facing the future with confidence and without God.

There are few who would endorse this symbolism today. The city is now often viewed as a symbol of decay and despair; of hopes dashed, of the inability of human beings to master their own destiny. Most New Yorkers might find it difficult to believe that their city could somehow represent or embody the hopes of the human race. To many of them, it represents the squalid side of human nature, bringing together in a concentrated and highly visible form the vices and shortcomings to which human nature is prone. The modern city is more of a witness to the nature and effects of structural sin than to the human ideals which are alleged to transcend such sin.

The image of the city is thus ambivalent. It does not only represent something purely positive, something which the believer is required to affirm and endorse uncritically. It can also represent the forces opposed both to constructive human existence and to the spiritual life. The world, although a creation of God, is a fallen creation, enslaved to sin. The image of the city firmly points to sin having communal, as well as individual, elements. Sin affects human structures and societies, as well as the individuals which comprise them. As Luther put it, 'We serve here below in an inn. The master of the house is the devil, the mistress of the house is the world, and all sorts of evil passions reign within it.' So a genuine problem develops: how can one affirm human society, without simultaneously affirming the structural sin which is endemic within it? How can one adopt a genuinely world-affirming spirituality, without endorsing all that is wrong with the world? It is clear that Christians are meant to live within the world. But how? To deploy a characteristic turn of phrase from the Fourth Gospel, Christians are meant to be in the world, yet not of the world (John 17). But how can this delicate balancing act be achieved?

Critically Affirming the World

The mainstream Reformation witnessed the rejection of two options which it believed were deeply inimical to authentic Christian existence within the world. In the first place, it dismissed one of the most powerfully world-affirming spiritualities which the Christian church has ever known – that of the Renaissance papacy. The Renaissance popes had no difficulties in affirming the world and its values and methods, occasionally even developing new twists. The Borgia pope Alexander vi was chiefly noted for his generous use of poison in getting rid of individuals who had attitude problems. Alexander turned dinner parties into a Renaissance version of Russian roulette: you were never quite sure which of the many dishes would contain a lethal dose of some noxious substance. Where Jesus counselled talking through difficulties with your opponents, Alexander favoured more direct and permanent approaches hitherto neglected by Christian spiritual directors. Leo x, the pope who condemned Luther in 1520, was a member of the prominent Florentine banking family of the Medicis, who had liquidated his bank in order to purchase the papacy outright. There were other, more suitable, candidates for the papacy at that point, most of whom had fewer mistresses and children than Leo, and occasionally even none. Leo was, by all accounts, a good-natured gourmet, equally fond of the worlds of high finance, hunting, and extravagant spending.

This spirituality had no problems, at either the theoretical or practical level, with sex, money or power. It knew how to get them, and it knew how to make the most of them. Its practitioners were generally deeply involved in affairs relating to them all. No-go areas were conspicuously absent. By its actions and attitudes, the Renaissance papacy showed that it affirmed the worldly order with confidence and *savoir faire*. There were no hang-ups evident at all. Here, it seems, was a world-affirming spirituality *par excellence*. Yet most Christians, even those firmly committed to the world, would feel decidedly uncomfortable with these attitudes. Those who affirm the world all too easily become those who have been mastered by the world. Most commentators – whether reformers or historians – regard the Renaissance papacy as a classic example of a degenerate and debauched version of Christianity, lacking authenticity and moral authority. To put it concisely: the world was affirmed at the price of negating the gospel. Those who thought they had conquered the world had actually been conquered by it.

If the Renaissance papacy showed up the inadequacy of an un-critical world-affirming spirituality, the reformers believed that shortcomings of a world-renouncing spirituality were equally evident by the late Middle Ages. For in the second place, the mainstream Reformation rejected the monastic impulse to withdraw from the world. An illustration will bring out this point. The most famous writing of the *Devotio Moderna* is Thomas à Kempis' *De Imitatione Christi*. The full title of this work, in English, is *On the Imitation of Christ and Contempt for the World*. A positive response to Jesus Christ entails a negative response to the world. For Thomas à Kempis, the world is essentially a nuisance. It distracts us from other-worldly contemplation. If the monk wishes to gain experience of the world, he need do nothing more than look around his cell. We are pilgrims upon earth, in the process of travelling to heaven; to develop a commitment to, or even an interest in, the present world is potentially to risk the goal of the entire monastic existence – holiness in the present world, and salvation in the future.

Similar attitudes can be instanced from other monastic move-ments, such as the Carthusians. The monk was to seek solitude, not merely from the world, but from other human beings. Whenever possible, he was to remain within his cell. William of St Thierry was one of many medieval spiritual writers who made puns on the Latin word for cell, *cella*. The cell hides (*celare*, the Latin root from which the English word 'conceal' is derived) the monk from the world, and opens up heaven (*coelum*) to the monk. Similar attitudes are associated with Geert Groote, widely regarded as the founder of the *Devotio Moderna*, who renounced all material possessions and academic pursuits, in order to withdraw totally from the world to seek God.

A variation on this option was proposed by the radical wing of the Reformation, often generally referred to as 'the Anabaptists'. Many of the radicals despaired of the secular order, regarding it as virtually beyond redemption. The world is evil. Holiness can only be maintained by totally withdrawing from society – a view which sociologists dub the 'sectarian' mentality or the 'privatisation of Christianity'. In particular, they rejected its social ordering, especially its coercive dimensions. The radicals incurred the intense dislike, perhaps even the fear, of the secular authorities through their refusal to own property, to carry arms, and to swear oaths.

This attitude towards the world was so critical that it proved impossible for the radicals to live within the world; small communities developed, not unlike the Amish of today, who withdrew from the world and its order. There is an obvious degree of similarity with medieval monasticism here. However, the radical communities embraced men and women of all ages. They reflected the make-up of secular society in every way, except that they rejected certain of its fundamental beliefs and practices. The extent of that rejection, however, made it virtually impossible for them to live in the common social order; they believed they should withdraw, and found their own. There are important parallels here with modern Evangelical subcultures, which often stress the importance of detaching oneself from the world, and existing only in a totally Christian background. To be a real Christian, you need to immerse yourself in a Christian subculture, and avoid any contact with the world.

Many of the reformers (especially Vadian at St Gallen) were deeply sympathetic to the motivation which they discerned as underlying monasticism. Many valued the spiritual literature which issued from some of the great monasteries of Europe. But even this appreciation was reluctantly mingled with criticism: one could not, and should not, withdraw from the world. Other reformers were harsher in their attitude towards the monasteries, noting that many had become lax in their ways and rich in their possessions. Erasmus commented caustically upon the sexual vices which he asserted to be rife within monasteries, as well as noting various other aspects of institutionalisation which rendered its subjects of strictly limited value to the everyday world.

But even amidst this more practical evaluation, a genuine theological anxiety is repeatedly expressed – to be a Christian is to be called to serve God within the world. There were to be no Protestant equivalents of the monasteries. A commitment to the world meant a commitment to live in the world, sharing its way of life, its risks and its opportunities. The potential of a *temporary* withdrawal from the world, for the purposes of spiritual renewal, was recognised by the reformers; the idea of a *permanent* withdrawal was, however, regarded as a misguided individualism, tantamount to an abrogation of one's Christian responsibilities.

To withdraw from the world, or to affirm the world from within? The tensions between these two different attitudes to the world – that which governed the past, and that which would govern the future – can be seen at work in history. As we have stressed throughout this work, to study the history of Christianity is to study spirituality embodied in history. An episode of the years 1510–11 illustrates the real spiritual crises which could be precipitated by uncertainty concerning one's attitude to the world.

During the first decade of the sixteenth century, a small group of young Italian nobility met regularly, in order to discuss matters of religion. The members of this group shared a common concern: to ensure the salvation of their souls. But how could this be done? In 1510, a crisis developed within the group. Eventually, one section came to the conclusion that the only way to ensure personal salvation was to withdraw totally from the world. The threat to personal holiness posed by the world could only be countered by isolation from it. This group withdrew to a local monastery, there to work out their salvation safe from the influences of a fallen world. The second group chose to remain in the world. Somehow, they reasoned, it must be possible to remain in the world, and attain salvation.

In 1957 the distinguished historian Hubert Jedin, rummaging through the archives of an Italian monastery, came across the letters of one member of this group, Gasparo Contarini. Contarini apparently maintained a regular correspondence with Paolo Giustiniani, the leader of the group who chose to seek salvation within the confines of the monastery. In these letters, Contarini reflects upon the agony of his situation, allowing us access to the spiritual torment which afflicted him in the aftermath of the decision of his friends to leave the world. Throughout late 1510 and early 1511, he explains how he is unable to justify his decision to remain in the world. How could he maintain integrity of faith, living in a city, while his former colleagues had submitted themselves to a spartan discipline and programme of personal austerity? Then, on Easter Eve 1511, Contarini relates how he happened to fall into conversation with an Evangelically minded Benedictine monk. (The Benedictine Order is now known to have been a centre for a form of Catholic Evangelicalism at the time.) The monk explained to Contarini that Christ, through his death on the cross, had gained the forgiveness of all of Contarini's sins. Contarini was exultant. 'I shall sleep and wake as securely as if I had spent my entire life in a monastery!' he wrote to his friend Giustiniani. Life in the world had been placed upon a secure theological foundation.

Now there is a very important observation to be made here. The ideas which Contarini encountered on Easter Eve 1511, would be developed and consolidated in the Reformation doctrine of justification by faith. This doctrine, so central to the Reformation, gave a theoretical justification to those who believed that they had been called by God to live out their Christian lives in the everyday world of the sixteenth century. The doctrine affirmed that it was not necessary, and not even desirable, to retreat to a monastery for salvation. Salvation was at hand for all who put their faith in God through Christ, and lived through faith. It was faith which mattered; the arena in which it was to be lived out was of minor importance. With the clear articulation of this decisive doctrine in the early 1520s, a new commitment to the world was possible, theoretically and practically. Faithfulness to the gospel was no longer understood to entail a withdrawal from the world. The doctrine of justification by faith affirmed the multiplicity of contexts open to Christian existence, laying a theoretical foundation for the positive living out of the Christian faith in the everyday world.

For such reasons, the mainstream, or magisterial, reformers countered both the monastic and the radical proposals with what they believed to be in the first place a more Christian, and in the second a more realistic, approach. This could be termed the *critical affirmation of the secular order*. You live in the world; you address yourself to it; you value it, in that it is the creation of God; but you also recognise that it is a fallen creation, in principle being capable of redemption. Just as God loves sinners, while cherishing the Christ-centred vision of those sinners as redeemed, so writers such as Calvin affirmed and addressed the fallen secular order, while holding out the vision of a reformed and redeemed society, worthy of the name of the city of God.

There is a dialectic in Calvin's thought between the world, as the creation of God himself, and the world as the fallen creation. In that it is God's creation, it is to be honoured, respected and affirmed; in that it is a fallen creation, it is to be criticised with the object of redeeming it. These two insights could be described as the twin foci of the ellipse of Calvin's world-affirming spirituality. A strong doctrine of creation prevents Calvin from lapsing into a hatred of the world, or a crude suggestion that everything in the world is evil. Calvin's constant stress upon the beauty of the creation, evident even to fallen humanity, tempers his doctrine of the fallenness of that creation. The world may be fallen – but it remains the beautiful creation of God, good in itself, and capable of being redeemed and restored. A similar pattern can be discerned in Calvin's doctrine of human nature, where – despite his stress upon the sinful nature of fallen humanity – Calvin never loses sight of the fact that it remains God's creation. Though stained by sin, it remains the creation and possession of God, and is to be valued for that reason.

Human society and civilisation, as they are embodied in the image of the city, are capable of being redeemed, of being brought into line with God's will – a notion which Calvin links specifically with the idea of 'order'. The God-given ordering of creation, though disrupted by sin, can be restored – and the means of that restoration is itself consistent with that original ordering (an important point in grasping the central concerns of Calvin's understanding of the meaning of the death of Christ). As Calvin states this in commenting upon Psalm 11:4: 'It is the glory of our faith that God, the creator of the world, in no way disregards the order which he first established.' For Calvin, for example, God's aim in redeeming society – rather than just individuals within it – is the creation of a loving and caring community, capable of attracting and assimilating outsiders, whose chief inhabitant and sole sustainer is none other than the living God himself. (As the Westminster Catechism would later put this, 'The chief end and duty of man is to love God and enjoy him for ever.')

The present task and the future goal of Christian activity within the world is the restoration of the divine ordering of humanity and society, after the image and likeness of God. Within Calvin's conception of the Christian life, faith is not an individual affair, orientated primarily towards the private spiritual world of the believer. To flee from the world is to flee from a creation of God. Rather, faith is and ought to be concerned with the restoration of the fallen creation to fellowship with its creator, a process of restoration and reordering in which Christian believers have a vital and necessary role to play. The Quaker writer William Penn captured this aspect of Reformation spirituality well when he wrote: 'True godliness does not turn men out of the world, but enables them to live better in it, and excites their endeavours to mend it.'

The theme of 'the reordering of a fallen creation' has deep roots in the Christian tradition, and Calvin may be regarded as developing ideas primarily associated with the political theology of Augustine of Hippo. For Augustine, God created the world – including its various personal, societal and environmental interrelationships – according to a definite pattern. Augustine uses the term 'rectitude' to designate this God-given pattern of relationships. According to Augustine, this network of relationships has been compromised and distorted by the effects of sin. Sin is not merely a personal affair, relating to individual human beings; it is a structural affair, affecting society as a whole. In the process of justification (which Augustine interprets as 'making right'), the restoration of the rectitude of creation is being initiated. The same concerns, linked with a similar framework of interpretation (although a slightly different vocabulary), may easily be discerned within Calvin's thought. For Calvin, through the death of Christ 'the whole world has been renewed, and all things restored to order'. Augustine and Calvin share a common rejection of any dualistic division between the private and public dimensions of the Christian life, and a common quest for a spirituality which achieves a *legitimate* synthesis of Christian existence and existence in the world.

The resurrection itself is seen as a final and dramatic reordering of the fallen human estate. What has become old and tarnished through sin is reordered and recomposed by its creator. Perhaps there are few finer statements of this belief than that due to one of Calvin's later disciples, Benjamin Franklin. As a youthful printer at Philadelphia, Franklin composed his own epitaph:

> The Body of
> B Franklin Printer
> (Like the Cover of an old Book
> Its Contents torn out
> And stript of its Lettering and Gilding)
> Lies here, Food for Worms.
> But the Work shall not be lost;
> For it will (as he believ'd) appear once more,
> In a new and more elegant Edition
> Revised and Corrected
> By the Author.

This theme of the restoration of the lost order of the creation resonates throughout Calvin's thought. Its practical consequences are significant. On the one hand, then, the Christian is thus propelled into the forefront of the struggle to bring human society into line with the will of God. On the other hand, however, human society and civilisation are perfectly capable of bringing the believer into line with its patterns. A world-affirming spirituality must therefore be capable of sustaining this engagement, while protecting the believer against collapsing into the world, and losing his or her distinctiveness. The Christian is to be encouraged to invest and immerse himself or herself in the world – but that world must be kept at a critical distance. Outward investment and commitment must be accompanied by inner detachment and the fostering of a critical attitude.

There are obvious and helpful parallels here with the existential philosophy of the German writer Martin Heidegger. For Heidegger, existence is about 'standing out', about being different from the inanimate objects and artifacts around us. The world can assume a dual function in relation to human existence. It can be the place in which we live, our 'play room' (*Spielraum*), the arena in which human existence is located. On the other hand, it can pose a threat to human existence, by providing the catalyst by which we may fall into the world and lose our human distinctiveness. In its positive sense, the world is thus the location of human existence; in its negative sense, it is a threat to that existence. Much the same sort of tension is noted in the Fourth Gospel, where 'the world' can assume both of these functions – the creation of God, which he loves and for which he sent Jesus Christ to die, and of which we are part; and the fallen creation of God, which threatens to destroy and overwhelm faith.

For the Christian to adopt a positive and affirming attitude to society and culture is thus a risky business. There is a genuine danger of the believer being overwhelmed by the forces of the world, which perennially attempt to seduce the Christian's commitment from the creator to the fallen creation itself. There is thus a need to structure one's theological defences in order to avoid this pitfall.

Calvin's impressive world-affirming spirituality may be said to rest upon affirming the utter ontological distinction between God and the world, while denying the possibility of separating them. The theme *distinctio sed non separatio*, which underlies so many aspects of Calvin's theology, reappears in his spirituality. A knowledge of God the creator cannot be isolated from knowledge of his creation. The importance of the creation derives from the one who created it; Christians are expected to show respect, concern and commitment for the world on account of a loyalty, obedience and love for God its creator. The world does not have a direct claim to such loyalty; it is an indirect claim, resting upon a recognition of the unique relation of origin which exists between God and his creation. In revering nature as God's creation, one is worshipping God, not worshipping nature.

This point deserves closer consideration. For Calvin, the creation reflects its creator at every point. Image after image is flashed in front of our eyes, as Calvin attempts to convey the multiplicity of ways in which the creation witnesses to its creator: it is like a visible garment, which the invisible God dons in order to make himself known; it is like a book, in which the name of the creator is written as its author; it is like a theatre, in which the glory of God is publicly displayed; it is like a mirror, in which the works and wisdom of God are reflected. At one point, Calvin can even allow that nature *is* God ('provided it is said reverently'), so close is the link between God and his creation.

This spirituality gives a new foundation and motivation to the study of the natural sciences. Medicine and astronomy are commended as means of learning more of the glory of God through the study of the intricacies of the creation – a point of no small importance in understanding why, for example, it was individuals deeply influenced by Calvin's ideas who would make such fundamental contributions to the natural sciences in the sixteenth and seventeenth centuries. The wisdom of the invisible God may be discerned within the wonderful ordering of his visible and tangible creation. The *Belgic Confession* (1561) made this point in the following words. Nature is 'before our eyes as a most beautiful book in which all created things, whether great or small, are as letters showing the invisible things of God to us.'

It also gives us a new motivation for *enjoying* nature. Although often portrayed as an ascetic killjoy, determined to stop believers enjoying themselves at any cost, Calvin has a genuine concern to stress that creation was fashioned in order that we might rejoice in it, rather than merely survive through it. Quoting Psalm 104:15, Calvin points out that God created wine that makes human hearts glad. Food does not merely allow us to survive – it tastes good. 'God not only provides for our necessities, and bestows upon us as much as we need for the everyday purposes of life – in his goodness, he deals still more generously with us, by cheering our hearts with wine and oil. Nature would certainly be satisfied with water to drink! The addition of wine is thus due to God's overflowing generosity.' Similarly, the rich and satisfying associations of wine are given new meaning through the communion service, as Calvin pointed out in the 1540 *Treatise on the Lord's Supper*:

> When we see wine set forth as a symbol of blood, we must reflect upon the benefits which wine imparts to the human body. We thus come to realise that these same benefits are imparted to us in a spiritual manner by the blood of Christ. These benefits are to nourish, refresh, strengthen and gladden.

Calvin develops this point at length in the *Institutes*, pointing out how we are able to appreciate and enjoy the good things of life. 'All things are made for us, in order that we may know and acknowledge their author, and celebrate his goodness towards us by giving him thanks.' To be a Christian does not, indeed cannot, mean a renunciation of the world; to renounce the world is to renounce the God who so wondrously created it. To stress this point once more: the world, though fallen, is not evil. Even in its fallenness, it possesses a beauty and charm which provides the Christian with a powerful motivation to restore it to its God-given original state. If the world is this beautiful when fallen, how much more lovely it will be when it is restored and redeemed.

Yet for all this beauty, the creation is not God. It is God's; it derives from God; it bears the stamp of his authorship at point after point. Yet God is not to be identified with his creation. We must rise above the world to its author, who cannot be reduced to the level of the mundane (although Calvin will point out that, in the incarnation, God chose to come down to this level). A theoretical and practical distinction must be made. A competent educationalist until his dying day, Calvin insists that the best way of teaching people (the *ordo docendi*) is to begin with the known, and proceed to the unknown. It is therefore only natural to begin a discussion of the invisible God from the known visible world (and Calvin here commends Paul's Areopagus sermon as a model of its kind). But God transcends his creation, and cannot be reduced to it. Indeed, Calvin echoes the basic position of the Reformation when he points out that, wrongly understood, creation can lead to idolatry – that is, to the worship and glorification of the creation, instead of the creator. There is thus a dual attitude to creation evident within Calvin's thought. Rightly understood, nature is something which originates from God, reflects his creative being, and is capable of pointing away from itself towards the one who created it. Wrongly understood, nature is capable of drawing us away from God, in that we lose sight of its creator and his purposes. It is painfully easy to lapse into a worship of the creation, under the misguided misapprehension that it *is* God.

Zwingli also stresses the real danger of confusing the creator and the creation, and coming to trust in and rely upon the latter, rather than the former. In a revealing comment, Zwingli explains to his readers how this point was brought home to him forcibly by reading a poem by Erasmus of Rotterdam.

My dear brothers and sisters in Christ, I do not wish to keep from you how I came to the opinion and firm belief that we need no mediator except Jesus Christ, and that there is none but Christ alone who can mediate between God and ourselves. Some eight or nine years ago, I read a comforting poem by the most learned Erasmus of Rotterdam, addressed to the Lord Jesus. In this poem, Jesus laments, in many beautiful words, that we do not seek all that is good from him – even though he is the source of all good; a saviour, comfort and treasure of the soul. Then I thought to myself: it is always like that. Why is it that we always seek help from the creature?

For Zwingli, true Christian spirituality depends upon a constant turning away from the natural human tendency to trust in creatures, and turning instead towards their source and origin in God. Zwingli's prayer to this effect remains helpful: 'Almighty God, grant that we may all recognise our blindness, and that we who have thus far clung to creatures may from now on cling to the creator, that he may be our only treasure, and that our heart may rest in him.'

Augustine of Hippo had anticipated much the same difficulty centuries earlier, when he observed in a sermon that 'we should not love the world, but must work within it in such a way that it does not seduce us.' A correct attitude to creation removes this difficulty. Calvin locates this attitude in a theoretical doctrinal framework which lays emphasis simultaneously upon the absolute distinction, yet practical inseparability, of God and his world. No fundamental divorce is possible between God and his world. They cannot be had in isolation from one another. Yet they are not the same. Calvin's achievement is to fashion a framework which allows the world to be affirmed in that it is *of* God, and kept at a critical distance in that it is *not* God.

Such insights, when linked with the doctrine of justification by faith, provide a sophisticated and intelligible theoretical foundation for the adoption of strongly positive and committed attitudes towards the world. Luther put this point as follows:

In every age, the saints live in the world in the following ways. They get on with domestic affairs and the everyday world, they carry on public business, they build families, they cultivate fields, and they become involved in commerce or some other sort of career. But they recognise that they, like their fathers, are strangers in exile; they use this world as a place of passage.

Elsewhere, Luther suggests that, 'in the purposes of God, this world is only a preparation and a scaffolding for the world to come.' In other words, its purpose is educational, a 'vale of soul-making' (Keats) which makes us fit and ready for its future counterpart. (Incidentally, such passages also serve to draw attention to the eschatological orientation of faith in the writings of the reformers, especially Luther: faith looks beyond the present world to its fulfilment in eternal life.)

In his *Geneva Catechism*, Calvin suggests the model of a tourist, as an illustration of the sort of attitude he wishes to commend. We are, Calvin suggests, 'to learn to pass through this world as though it is a foreign country, treating all earthly things lightly and declining to set our hearts upon them'. In other words, we are encouraged to enjoy, respect and explore the world – while realising that it is not our home.

> All things that are connected with the enjoyment of the present life are sacred gifts of God. If we abuse them, however, we pollute them. Why? Because we always dream of staying in this world – with the result that those things which were meant to help us pass through it instead become hindrances to us, in that they hold us fast to the world. So it was not without good reason that Paul, wishing to arouse us from this stupidity, calls upon us to consider the brevity of this life, and suggests that we ought to treat all the things of this life as if we did not own them. For if we recognise that we are strangers in the world, we will use the things of this world as if they belong to someone else – that is, as things that are lent to us for a single day.

Calvin draws on a range of images, such as the Old Testament theme of 'exile from a homeland', in developing this point: the world cannot be allowed to dominate our spiritual horizons. To anticipate one of Gadamer's phrases, we must attempt to achieve a fusion of the horizons of time and eternity, of the world that is and the world that is to come, in order that the Christian hope of resurrection and eternal life may inform our thinking and acting in human history and society. We are to develop 'a contempt of the present life which gives rise to no hatred for it or ingratitude towards God'. Ascetic devaluation of the present life has, for Calvin, no place whatsoever in the Christian mindset. The transiency of the present life is an incentive to make the most of it – but always in the knowledge that it cannot be compared to what is to come. To show too great a commitment to the present world is potentially to deny the reality of eternal life, to which the present is a pointer.

Perhaps one of the finest statements of this attitude, as applied to the North American situation, may be found in Jonathan Edwards' sermon 'The Christian Pilgrim'. Edwards' faithful application of his Calvinist heritage to his situation could be summarised in one of that sermon's most direct statements: 'It was never designed by God that this world should be our home.' Speaking with the eighteenth-century situation in New England in mind, Edwards declared:

> Though surrounded with outward enjoyments, and settled in families with desirable friends and relations; though we have companions whose society is delightful, and children in whom we see many promising qualifications; though we live by good neighbors and are generally beloved where known; yet we ought not to take our rest in these things as our portion . . . We ought to possess, enjoy and use them, with no other view but readily to quit them, whenever we are called to it, and to change them willingly for heaven.

In the light of the Christian hope of resurrection and eternal life, the present life is revealed as a means, rather than an end; a prologue, rather than a book in itself; an overture, rather than an opera. Calvin's fundamental criticism of those who uncritically immerse themselves in the world is that they treat something provisional and transitory as if it were absolute and permanent. As the Christian begins to gain foretastes and foresights of what the world to come is like, he or she will gradually come to see the present life as the good, to which the life to come is the better. The present life is 'a gift of God's kindness', to be welcomed and received *and enjoyed* – both for what it is in itself, and for its intimations and hints of what is yet to come.

The World, Theology and Spirituality

One of the most pressing problems at the time of the Reformation concerned the extent to which secular ideas could be allowed to impose upon religious ideas. For many writers, the sixteenth century witnessed the birth of secular humanism. While it is absurd to suggest that a no-God ideology became a serious alternative to Christianity at the period, hints of this important feature of modern western thought may unquestionably be discerned in the later Italian Renaissance. It became increasingly commonplace for Zeus, Jupiter and the 'God of the Christians' (to borrow a phrase from Tertullian) to be merged into one another, and seen as representing the moral and spiritual qualities of classical civilisation – Hellenic, Roman and Hebraic. The origins of this trend might be traced back to Collucio Salutati, who suggested that the gods of antiquity could be 'demythologised' (if I could use a twentieth-century term), and regarded purely as embodiments of virtues. The same process appears to have been extended to Christianity by the beginning of the sixteenth century, if the reports of Erasmus of Rotterdam are to be relied upon.

Charles Trinkaus, a leading authority on the religious aspects of the Renaissance, has written that 'the secularisation of culture and the "deification" of man grew directly out of the movements and attitudes that were present within medieval-Renaissance-Reformation Christianity itself . . . what was going on was a tendency to secularise the sacred while simultaneously sacralising the secular.' In the chapter which follows, we shall see how the Reformation work ethic 'sacralises the secular' by giving ordinary work a new religious status and motivation; it is now necessary to consider the other side of this particular coin – the tendency to reduce the religious to the secular. There can be no doubt that cultural developments during the period of the later Renaissance gave a new urgency to the quest for a means of preventing the sacred from collapsing into the secular.

In the modern period, two options have emerged as appropriate for dealing with the interaction of Christian faith and the secular world. On the one hand, we have what I shall call 'the theology of the barricade', which resolutely refuses to allow any interaction between an allegedly pure theology and the contamination of the secular world. I choose the image of the

barricade to suggest a type of interface which is meant to pre-
clude any passage of persons or ideas. Faith and the world are
opposing forces, to be kept apart at all costs. Theological purity
is maintained at the price of a near-total inability to address
the world outside its self-appointed – and heavily barricaded –
enclosure. It is a defensive form of spirituality, similar to the
Boer *kraal*, maintained by a siege mentality. Its authenticity
is judged by the extent to which secular ideas and values are
excluded from every area of faith.

Rebecca Manley Pippert captures this attitude perfectly in
her work *Out of the Saltshaker*, when she writes:

> There is also confusion about what it means to be spiritual. We
> feel that it is more spiritual to take our non-Christian roommate
> to a bible study or to church than to a play or out for pizza. Just
> as we do not understand our natural points of contact with the
> world, we don't understand our natural points of contact with
> God himself. He made us human. He is therefore interested
> in our humanness. We dare not limit him to bible studies and
> discussions with Christians. He created life, and he desires to
> be glorified in the totality of all that adds up to life.

On the other hand, we have what I shall designate the
'theology of posture', which assumes that Christian integrity
and relevance are best safeguarded by making Christianity
indistinguishable from the world. This can take the form of
erecting an entire theological (although the use of that word
is a little inappropriate, as there is often little obvious place
for God) foundation upon a contemporary cultural idea or value,
without any reference to the historic resources of the Christian
tradition. Liberal theology and spirituality is little more than a
transient agglomerate of attitudes and ideas, deriving directly
from its secular environment. It is this secular environment,
rather than the resources of the Christian tradition, which is
seen as the primary stimulus, motivating force and guiding
principle of liberal spirituality.

Christian theology and spirituality thus become like chameleons, blending into the cultural background in such a way that
they lose their distinctiveness. And like chameleons, they don't

get noticed. They don't stand out from the background. They are overlooked. This approach gauges its authenticity by its capacity to show how theology conforms to – or, even better, anticipates – the latest social and intellectual fashions of socially acceptable groups.

Perhaps these characterisations may seem to be caricatures. But the essence of a caricature is that it bears a recognisable resemblance to the real thing. And I write as one who once stood firmly within that second school of thought. In any case, the point I want to make is simple. Both these approaches fail to get noticed – the first on account of a total failure to address the world, the second because of an innate inability to stand out from the world. Both are thoroughly well-intentioned in their approaches. Both have laudable goals – yet the irony of the situation is that both have miscarried.

The approach commended (and adopted) by Calvin is sufficiently specific as to allow us to define its contours, while sufficiently flexible to allow us to transfer it from the limiting conditions of his situation to those of today. The basic assumption is the following: the Christian faith itself, especially in its doctrinal respects, offers us a framework for living and believing. It is this framework of a vital and rigorously informed faith which allows the believer to identify and withstand the social and intellectual forces which might pose a lethal threat to the Christian faith.

Nevertheless, not every social and intellectual force poses a threat to the Christian faith. An informed faith – that is to say, a faith which does not merely believe, but which believes certain quite definite things, which it grounds in Scripture and the Christian tradition – is capable of exercising discrimination in these respects. It is able to be critical of developments around it, and evaluate them. It refuses to adopt the simplistic and dangerous positions, which either treat every development in secular culture as satanic and destructive on the one hand, or God-given and authoritative on the other. It is able to articulate criteria by which such developments may be judged. Christian theology is always the major premise of this evaluative syllogism.

It is natural that Christian theology and spirituality should show a keen and informed interest in developments in the secular world – whether philosophical (such as existentialism) or psychological (such as Jungian analysis). But in the end, it must actively evaluate, rather than passively accept, their commendations. Christian theology and spirituality are at their weakest and at their most bankrupt when they merely assimilate such developments, obliging future generations to undo their work.

I can still remember a lecture at Oxford which seemed to bring out this point with considerable clarity. I had to introduce a visiting speaker from the United States, whose theme was something like 'Liberation and Culture'. It was not a particularly good lecture, but its basic theme was that modern culture was setting the pace which Christian theology ought to follow. Where culture went, we ought to go as well. Afterwards, we had some time for discussion. No one wanted to ask any questions. To give people time to think of questions to put to the speaker, I asked him one myself. 'You seem to be saying that the way things are is the way things are meant to be – or that the way things will be is right. Doesn't this rob us of any possibility of judging culture? Of suggesting that culture can occasionally take wrong turnings, which need to be criticised and corrected?' It was an obvious question, which I fully expected him to have thought through.

There was a pause, which soon became an embarrassing silence. I cannot remember the precise words that the speaker then used; but I can remember the shockingly negative impact that they had on me and the remainder of his audience. For the substance of that reply was: 'I guess you might be right there.' There was no criteriology, no way of allowing Christianity to judge culture – whereas culture, according to this speaker, had every right to judge Christianity on the basis of its criteria.

The recognition of the need to adopt a critical approach to the world is not a decision to adopt a uniformly negative approach to human culture. This would be as misguided and out of place as a totally positive approach, lacking the will or ability to recognise elements of culture which are potentially opposed to the gospel. In his influential book *The Poverty of Historicism*, Karl Popper made the following criticism of Marxism: it appears to assume that the coming order is the only acceptable morality. The values of the future, because they are inevitable, are right. Its morality is based upon the fact that it is going to happen, whether we like it or not. Although it is difficult to find anyone prepared to defend the notion of the inevitability of socialism nowadays, Popper's point remains valid: just because something happens, or is alleged to be about to happen, doesn't make it *right*. And so theology needs to be able to criticise cultural developments. It needs to ask hard questions before accepting the latest cultural package on offer.

The Reformation offers us a proposal for adopting a critical yet affirmative attitude to the world; it still has much to commend it. If we are to accept it, we must make available opportunities for Christians to engage in serious and sustained theological reflection. The rich treasures of the spirituality and theology of the Christian church must be made available and accessible. They cannot be allowed to collect dust, unused, in the bank vaults of a defensive orthodoxy, nor can they be debased through an uncritical amalgamation with whatever aspect of modern culture happens to meet with our approval. They must be removed from those vaults, and forged into modern coinage – genuine, not counterfeit, Christian coinage. The Reformation itself attempted to undertake such a programme of theological and spiritual education, making its people articulate and informed in the apprehension and application of their faith. History offers us a vision of possibilities; perhaps there is room to begin to act on its basis. The spirituality of work developed by the reformers is a case in point, as will become clear in the chapter which follows.

7   Faith in the Everyday World: The Dignity of Human Work

In the previous chapter, we explored how the reformers developed a sophisticated spirituality which allowed believers to live out active lives in the world, without losing sight of the fact that the Christian hope is firmly directed towards eternal life. The impact of this positive approach to Christian life in the world may also be seen in what is perhaps one of the most important contributions of Reformation spirituality to the shaping of modern western culture – the work ethic.

The phrase 'the Protestant work ethic' is probably as well known as its basic ideas are misunderstood. A 'work ethic' continues to occupy a significant position within modern western culture, especially in the United States – witness President Richard Nixon's famous Labor Day address, in which he concluded that

> America's competitive spirit, the work ethic of this people, is alive and well on Labor Day, 1971. The dignity of work, the value of achievement, the morality of self-reliance – none of these is going out of style.

Given the importance of this idea, it is clearly helpful to return to its origins. Modern variants upon, or accounts of, the original Protestant work ethic are often considerably removed from both

its spirit and its substance. Perhaps the most radical departure is
that so enthusiastically commended by Nixon – 'the morality of
self-reliance', to which we shall return presently. Let us begin
by exploring the Reformation approach to work.

The Protestant Work Ethic

To appreciate the significance of the Reformation work ethic, it
is necessary to understand the intense distaste with which the
early Christian tradition, illustrated by the monastic writers,
regarded work. For Eusebius of Caesarea, the perfect Christian
life was one devoted to serving God, untainted by physical
labour. Those who chose to work for a living were second-rate
Christians. To live and work in the world was to forfeit a
first-rate Christian calling, with all that this implied. The early
monastic tradition appears to have inherited this attitude, with
the result that work often came to be seen as a debasing and
demeaning activity, best left to one's social – and spiritual –
inferiors. If the social patricians of ancient Rome regarded work
as below their status, it has to be said that a spiritual aristocracy
appears to have developed within early Christianity, with equally
negative and dismissive attitudes towards manual labour. Such
attitudes probably reached their height of influence during the
Middle Ages.

If the medieval period knew of a work ethic, it was often
predominantly negative in its tone: work did not always interfere
with establishing a perfect relationship with God. The slogan
laborare est orare, 'to work is to pray', summarised the conviction
of some (but not all) religious orders that the contemplative life
was not necessarily destroyed by occasional manual labour. The
monk's dedication to a lifetime of contemplation and prayer was
not necessarily compromised by spending some time in humiliating and degrading manual work, such as tending the monastery's
vineyard, or supervising other aspects of its worldly affairs.

'Work', however, was firmly understood as action within
the confines of monastic life – it was not life in the everyday
world. For orders such as the Carthusians, work was firmly
understood as 'activity which can be carried out within the

monk's cell' (the copying of texts being a particular favourite). Indeed, some monastic writers commended work as an aid to humility. Work was demeaning and degrading, the sort of thing which no respectable person would consider doing. By working, the monk undertook something painful and humiliating as a way of purging his soul.

Monastic spirituality was widely perceived to treat work as degrading, as the writings of Erasmus of Rotterdam indicate. There was just no way in which most monastic spirituality allowed that the ordinary Christian, living out his or her life in the everyday world, could be regarded as pursuing a religious calling, or as having a claim to be a first-class Christian (if this distinction was held to be of any importance). Christians who committed themselves to living and working in the everyday world were, by definition, second-rate Christians. As Adriano Tilgher concluded in his definitive study of work in the western world, monastic spirituality never regarded everyday work in the world as anything of value. Those who chose to live and work in the world were merely at best 'regarded with indulgent charity'. Work was, in short, not a serious option for a *real* Christian. Erasmus reacted with scorn to this idea: was not the work of the humble ploughman more pleasing to God than monastic ritual?

The Reformation witnessed a dramatic reversal of this way of thinking. As we have seen, the reformers rejected the vital medieval distinction between the 'sacred' and 'secular'. There was no genuine difference of status between the 'spiritual' and the 'temporal' order (see p. 27). All Christians were called to be priests – and that calling extended to the everyday world. Christians were called to be priests to the world, purifying and sanctifying its everyday life from within. Luther stated this point succinctly: 'What seem to be secular works are actually the praise of God and represent an obedience which is well pleasing to him.' There were no limits to this notion of calling. Luther even extolled the religious value of housework, declaring that although it had 'no obvious appearance of holiness, yet these very household chores are more to be valued than all the works of monks and nuns'. Luther's English follower William Tyndale commented that while the 'washing of dishes and preaching the word of God' represented different human activities, he went on to insist that 'as touching to please God', there was no difference.

Underlying this new attitude is the notion of the 'calling'. God calls his people, not just to faith, but to express that faith in quite definite areas of life. One is called, in the first place, to be a Christian, and in the second, to live out that faith in a quite definite sphere of activity within the world. Whereas monastic spirituality regarded vocation as a calling *out* of the world into the seclusion and isolation of the monastery, Luther and Calvin regard vocation as a calling *into* the everyday world.

God calls believers, not merely to faith, but also to an arena of activity within his world. The idea of a 'calling' or *vocation* is first and foremost about being called by God, to serve him within his world. Work was thus seen as an activity by which Christians could deepen their faith, leading it on to new qualities of commitment to God. The Christian calling was a call to commitment to and action within the world. Activity within the world, simultaneously motivated, informed and sanctioned by Christian faith, was the supreme means by which the believer could demonstrate his or her commitment and thankfulness to God. To do anything for God, and to do it well, were the fundamental hallmarks of authentic Christian faith – whether, according to Tyndale, the task is keeping sheep or preaching the word of God. Diligence and dedication in one's everyday life are a proper response to God.

'Every individual's way of life is, as it were, a position assigned to him by the Lord.' For Calvin, God places individuals where he wants them to be. (This point, incidentally, is of importance to Calvin's critique of human ambition, which he argues rests upon an unwillingness to accept the sphere of action which God has allocated to us.) The social status of this location is an irrelevance, a human invention of no spiritual importance. One cannot allow the human evaluation of the status of an occupation to be placed above the judgement of God. All human work is capable of 'appearing truly respectable and being considered highly important in the sight of God'. No occupation, no calling, is too mean or lowly to be graced by the presence of God. As the English reformer, Hugh Latimer, put this point:

> Our Saviour Christ . . . was a carpenter, and got his living with great labour. Therefore let no man disdain . . . to follow him in a common calling and occupation. For as he blessed our nature with taking upon him the shape of man, so in his doing he blessed all occupations and arts.

The work of believers is thus seen to possess a significance which goes far beyond the visible results of that work. It is the person who works, as much as the resulting work, which is a thing of significance in the sight of God. There is no distinction between spiritual and temporal, sacred and secular work. All human work, however lowly, is capable of glorifying God. Work is, quite simply, an act of praise – a potentially *productive* act of praise. As Luther remarked, 'The whole world could be filled with the service of God – not just the churches, but the home, the kitchen, the cellar, the workshop and the fields.' Significantly, Luther and Calvin both noted the importance of productive activity for Christian self-esteem. By doing things for God, Christians are able to gain a sense of satisfaction and self-esteem, unattainable by other means.

It is commonplace for modern western analysts, whose assumptions are deeply moulded by secular values deriving both from capitalism and from its critics, to treat work as 'paid labour'. An excellent example of this trend is provided by Kornhauser's study *The Mental Health of the Industrial Worker* (1965). In evaluating the importance of work for his subjects, Kornhauser rigorously excluded any activity other than paid labour from his conception of 'work'. The Detroit automobile worker was said to 'work' when he was paid to assemble automobiles, and not to work when he worked, without pay, in his garden or home. This prejudicial evaluation is absent from the Reformation work ethic. For the reformers, work is not to be equated with paid employment; rather, it is human activity in the world, undertaken to please and serve God, irrespective of its remuneration or the value placed upon it by society.

If there are important differences between the reformers and the industrial society concerning the nature of work, there are perhaps even more fundamental differences concerning its motivation. The important study *The Work Ethic in Industrial America 1850–1920* states the motivating principles of a secular work ethic as follows:

> The central premise of the work ethic was that work was the core of moral life. Work made men useful in a world of economic scarcity. It staved off the doubts and temptations that preyed on idleness, it opened the way to deserved wealth and status, it allowed one to put the impress of mind and skill on the material world.

For the reformers, however, the ultimate motivation of human activity was to be located in a God-ward direction. The particular emphasis might differ from one reformer to another, but the underlying theme is constant: work is a natural response to God's gracious initiative towards us, by which we demonstrate our thankfulness to him, and simultaneously glorify and serve him in his world. Culturally conditioned notions of social utility are relativised by this over-riding concern. Work is something which glorifies God; it is something which serves the common good; it is something through which human creativity can express itself. The last two, it must be stressed, are embraced by the first. As Calvin's English follower William Perkins put it, 'The true end of our lives is to do service to God in serving of man.'

This insight is important in assessing some aspects of the Reformation work ethic. Calvin, for example, weighs in strongly in support of St Paul's injunction, 'If someone does not work, then he should not eat' (2 Thessalonians 3:10). Perhaps with memories of the shocking social conditions of the 1920s in mind, several modern writers have severely criticised Calvin for doing so, feeling that his comments demonstrate him to have been insensitive to the needs of the unemployed. Calvin's primary target, however, appears to have been quite different: the French aristocrats who sought refuge in Geneva, and felt that their social status placed them above the need to work. They *would* not work; for Calvin, the common human obligation is to labour in the garden of the Lord, in whatever manner is commensurate with one's God-given gifts and abilities on the one hand, and the needs of the situation on the other. The common obligation to work is the great social leveller, a reminder that all human beings are created equal by God.

The historical transformation of the status of work through this ethic is quite remarkable. In his magisterial study of the status of work from Aristotle to Calvin, *Il concetto di lavoro da Aristotele a Calvino*, Vittorio Tranquilli showed how Calvin's theology led directly from a view of work as a socially demeaning, if pragmatically necessary, activity, best left to one's social inferiors, to a dignified and glorious means of praising and affirming God in and through his creation, while adding further to its well-being. It is no accident that those regions of Europe which adopted Protestantism soon found themselves prospering economically – a spin-off, rather than an intended and premeditated consequence, of the new religious importance attached to work.

The Protestant work ethic is nowadays often described as an 'ethic of self-reliance' – witness Richard Nixon's words, quoted earlier. The implication is that the Reformation gave birth to the idea that people should pull themselves up by their own bootlaces. The notion of the self-made person is thus seen to be an integral part of the work ethic. In fact, however, this amounts to a serious misunderstanding of the original Reformation work ethic. The reformers continually stressed that we are what we are by the grace of God, not by dint of human effort. The notion of an achievement-centred spirituality was alien to the reformers, who mounted a sustained and radical critique of the theological foundations of the idea. In fact, the idea of the 'self-made person' is not due to the Reformation; it was a phenomenon already in existence in the cities of the early sixteenth century. The reformers had to address the idea and the reality of the 'self-made person'; they did not create it. Their task was to show that the gospel was relevant to such people, in the light of the consistent medieval monastic insistence that they were at best second-rate Christians, if they were Christians at all. So important is the Reformation critique of spiritualities of achievement, and so relevant is it to modern western society, that we shall devote the two chapters which follow to this matter.

We could summarise the Reformation attitude to work as follows. In serving our fellow human beings, we are glorifying God. Work is an act of praise. There is a God-given dignity to human work. By giving of our best in all our actions – whether it is playing the piano, writing books, tending our garden or living amongst the poor of the cities of the Third World – we are putting our faith into action, and glorifying the God who has called us. To become a Christian does not entail withdrawing from the world, but committing oneself to that world with a new outlook and a new quality of dedication – and achieving a quiet satisfaction in so doing, knowing that one is serving the Lord.

Modern Evangelicalism and the Retreat from the World

And it is at this point that modern Evangelicalism has lost sight of this foundational Reformation insight. In his recent survey of younger Evangelical students, entitled *Evangelicalism: The Coming Generation*, James Davison Hunter concluded that work has completely lost the significance it possessed for earlier generations. 'Work has lost any spiritual and eternal significance, and is important only in so far as it fosters certain qualities of the personality.' Evangelicalism needs to recover the notion of the spiritual dignity of work. The work ethic has become reduced to 'working for the weekend'. The Reformation simultaneously pointed behind and ahead with its attitude to work – behind to Scripture, and ahead to the future. Biblical attitudes to work and labour proved relevant and applicable to the early modern period. They still make a lot of sense today.

For the sad truth is that much modern Evangelicalism has become locked into the restricted and stale backwaters of a Christian subculture. Contacts with the secular world are often frowned upon. Yet Christians are meant to be *in* the world. They are meant to be witnessing to that world – and that implies a presence within the world. Christians are called to be salt and light *in* the world – not to withdraw from it totally. The love of God initially calls us out of the world – and then propels us back into it. The Christian doctrine of calling stresses that we are called to serve God *in the world*. Witness to the world from the safety of an isolated Christian enclave lacks real credibility.

The Reformation work ethic provides a vital – yet neglected – framework by which Christians can live out their lives in the world with integrity and commitment. You can serve the Lord, glorify his name, and bear witness to his love *by staying and working in the world*. Authentic witness to the world means involvement in that world. Work is an act of praise, and potentially an act of witness. By bringing a new dedication and depth to your work, you can witness while you work. It is *conforming* to the world, not *participating* in the world, which is worldly.

And it is here that the community of faith comes into its own. For such a commitment to the world involves a risk – a risk that, by being deeply immersed in the world, Christians will lose their distinctiveness, morale and vitality. The community of faith provides a vital network of support and nourishment for those committed to the world. It is like an oasis, providing refreshment for those who venture into the arid desert of the world. We shall be exploring this matter further in a later chapter.

But our attention is now claimed by a real problem for any Christian spirituality which wishes to address and engage with modern western society, arising directly from the importance attached to work in the everyday world. 'You are what you make yourself.' 'You have to pull yourself up by your own bootstraps.' Slogans such as these, which are the common coinage of achievement-orientated western culture, pose difficulties for a gospel of grace. How can we get the balance right between the grace of God and human achievement? With such questions, we move on to consider a cluster of issues at the heart of the Reformation struggle to reform and revitalise the Christian church – the doctrines of the grace of God, and of justification by faith.

8   Grace Abounding: Rediscovering the Graciousness of God

Having had to read countless undergraduate essays on the theme of 'the grace of God', I have reluctantly come to the conclusion that it is one of the most difficult Christian ideas to handle. The importance of the notion seems to be directly proportional to its complexity. Exasperated by my insistence that he define the idea, one of my students once retorted, 'I may not *understand* grace – but I believe in it profoundly!' What does that deceptively simple word 'grace' actually mean? How are we to think of it? How can we illustrate it? For the word 'grace' seems to denote something abstract and impersonal, an ill-defined and abstruse concept without any relation to the realities of human life. It is perhaps the abstract quality of this idea of grace that makes it so difficult to discuss.

During the Middle Ages, grace tended to be understood as a supernatural substance, infused by God into the human soul in order to facilitate redemption. One of the arguments underlying this approach went like this: There is a total and unbridgeable gap between God and human nature. There is no way that human beings can enter into a meaningful relation with God, on account of this gap. Something is needed to bridge this gap before we can be accepted by God.

Grace was therefore understood as something created within us by God, which acted as a bridge between pure human nature and divine nature – a kind of middling species. The notion of grace – or, more strictly, a created habit of grace – was thus regarded as some sort of bridgehead or middle ground, by which the otherwise absolute gulf between God and humanity could be bridged. Such ideas of grace had been the subject of severe criticism before the Reformation; by the beginning of the sixteenth century, they had largely fallen into disrepute.

Nonetheless, the way was still open for this notion to be conceived inadequately, in impersonal and abstract terms. This potential misunderstanding was eliminated by an understanding of the relation of grace and the action of the Holy Spirit which allowed grace to be understood, not merely as the graciousness of God, but as the dynamic and creative expression of this graciousness in human existence.

Grace: An Idea Recovered

The reformers, sensitive to the meaning of the Greek text of the New Testament, argued that the fundamental meaning of 'grace' was nothing other than the gracious favour of God towards us. It did not denote a substance; it designated God's personal attitude towards us. It did not refer to something which, so to speak, could be detached from God (such as a divine substance); rather, it represented a crucial dynamic aspect of the person of God. The strongly personal connotations of grace were thus recovered by the reformers. To speak of grace is to speak of the graciousness of God, as expressed in his dealings with us.

If I were to speak of a friend of mine as being 'kind', I would have to justify that statement by pointing to actions on his or her part illustrating that kindness. Kindness is not some sort of disembodied idea, but a personal attitude or quality which expresses itself in the way in which we relate to other people. Kindness, like grace, is something which declares itself in life.

Grace designates a pattern of divine presence and activity which we recognise as gracious. Though we are sinners, God is willing to meet us. Though we are deaf, God is willing to make himself heard. Though we are far away from him, God is willing to come to us, and bring us home to him. Though Christ was rich, yet for our sakes he became poor. Such themes recur throughout the writings of the Reformation, as its thinkers attempted to fathom and convey the depths of the grace of God.

To illustrate this point, we may pick up incidents in the lives of Luther, Calvin and Zwingli (to note only three of the more prominent representatives of the Reformation) which were attributed to the grace of God. The point we wish to make is the following: to speak of grace is to speak of changed human lives. Grace is known by its effects. God's attitude towards us is expressed in his actions towards us.

The young Luther was intensely aware of his personal sinfulness. Born in 1483, Luther entered the Augustinian monastery at the university city of Erfurt in 1505. Although meticulous in confession of his sins (which he later related to be numerous), he felt profoundly ill at ease within himself. His conscience was severely troubled by these sins, which he felt he was personally incapable of overcoming. It seemed to him that he was trapped in a sinful situation, from which there was no escape. Like a narcotics addict, he was hooked. There was no way he could break free from sin.

But how could a righteous God overlook such sin? Luther had especial difficulties with the phrase 'the righteousness of God', particularly as it was used by Paul. Indeed, at one point (Romans 1:16–17), Paul virtually equated the gospel with the revelation of the righteousness of God. This was beyond Luther's comprehension. How could the revelation of the righteousness of God be good news for sinners? It seemed to Luther that the gospel was good news for righteous persons – but for sinners, such as himself, the gospel meant one thing, and one thing only. God in his righteousness would punish and condemn sinners – including Martin Luther. In a piece of writing dating from 1545, the year before his death, Luther recalled the spiritual agony which gripped him during this early period.

> I hated that phrase 'the righteousness of God' . . . by which God is righteous, and punishes sinners. Although I lived an irreproachable life as a monk, I felt that I was a sinner, with an uneasy conscience in the sight of God . . . I was angry with

God, saying to myself, 'It's bad enough that miserable sinners should be condemned for ever by original sin, with all kinds of extra burdens laid upon us by the Old Testament law – and God makes things even worse through the gospel!

Then the situation was transformed. Probably about the year 1515, Luther came to the realisation that God was indeed able to forgive sins – including his own. He began to read Scripture in a completely new light. No longer did terms such as 'the righteousness of God' cause him to panic. They now resonated with the theme of the grace of God. The righteousness of God was not the righteousness by which God punished sinners, but the righteousness which God gave to sinners as a totally unmerited gift, in order that they might find solace and peace in him. It was as if he had entered into paradise, Luther later recalled.

> I began to understand that 'righteousness of God' as the righteousness by which righteous people live by the gift of God (in other words, faith), and the sentence 'the righteousness of God is revealed' to mean a passive righteousness, by which the merciful God justifies us by faith . . . This immediately made me feel as if I had been born all over again, and entered into paradise through open gates. From that moment onwards, the whole face of Scripture appeared to me in a different light . . . And, where I had once hated that phrase 'the righteousness of God' I now began to love it and praise it as the sweetest of words, so that this passage in Paul became the very gate of paradise for me.

Grace, for Luther, thus came to refer to a cluster of related ideas, all with a direct relevance to life. Above all, it referred to the astonishing fact that God loves sinners. Our status before God is something given, not something earned. 'Sinners are attractive because they are loved; they are not loved because they are attractive.' The amazing grace of God is shown in that we are loved before we are made lovable. To speak of the grace of God is to proclaim the astonishing insight that, despite the stranglehold which sin has upon us, God is able to break its power and purge its guilt – giving birth to a peaceful conscience and peace of mind.

To speak about grace is thus to speak about its effects in one's own life. God's gracious attitude towards us expresses itself in his gracious actions towards us. Grace cannot be isolated from its effects in our spiritual lives. A similar reflection can be detected in the writings of Paul in the New Testament, where the word 'grace' is often grounded in an account of the practical outworking of grace in his life – such as his conversion. Much the same point is made by John Bunyan, in his remarkable (and significantly titled) autobiography *Grace Abounding*.

A related note is struck by Huldrych Zwingli, the reformer of the Swiss city of Zurich. Born in 1484, Zwingli celebrated his thirty-fifth birthday (1 January 1519) by taking up a new job as people's priest (*Leutpriest*) at the Great Minster at Zurich. Within weeks, he was preaching a programme of reform which would eventually have considerable impact in the region. In addition to preaching, Zwingli also took on regular pastoral duties within the city. By the late summer of that year, Zwingli was close to death.

The plague had struck Zurich that summer, and Zwingli found himself heavily occupied with the visiting and consolation of the dying. Perhaps as many as a third of the population of the city died during this period. By August, Zwingli himself was seriously ill, and apparently was not expected to live. He wrote a poem during this period, in which he expressed his feeling of total dependence upon God. Whether he lived or died was a matter for God. It lay totally beyond human control.

Zwingli recovered. For him, the word 'grace' now resonated with tones of divine providence and omnipotence. Grace referred to God's willingness and ability to guide the course of human existence, to intervene in situations which lay beyond human control. If grace referred primarily to finding favour in the sight of God, it referred secondarily to the practical outworking of this in human life (and Zwingli had his preservation from the Zurich plague in mind). Once more, we find the same pattern: grace is about God's dynamic and creative involvement in the lives of those towards whom he is gracious.

John Calvin, born in 1509, may have had some early ambition to become a Catholic priest. The career possibilities open to

him were considerable: his father was a prominent ecclesiastical administrator at the cathedral city of Noyon, and Calvin
had developed cordial relations with the powerful de Hangest
family, known locally for their abundant powers of ecclesiastical
patronage. But by 1529, this possibility seemed closed. Calvin's
father had fallen out of favour with the cathedral, apparently over
some financial disagreement. Calvin, who had by now graduated
from the university of Paris, decided to study law instead of
theology. Perhaps the career prospects were better.

But although he successfully qualified as a lawyer, Calvin
began to develop an interest in and sympathy with the new
Evangelical ideas then sweeping through France. At some point,
probably in late 1533 or early 1534, Calvin underwent an experience which he would later refer to as a 'sudden conversion'. He
recalled how he seemed to be set in his ways, firmly entrenched
in the familiar and consoling paths of the old religion. And then
something happened. He does not explain precisely what, nor
is he generous with historical references, which might allow us
to establish precisely when all this took place. But the basic
patterns are clear. God intervened in his life, enabling him to
break with his old religious ways, and setting him free for the
service of the gospel. He saw himself as a stick-in-the-mud,
whom God extricated from dependence upon the old ways.
God 'subdued' him, in much the same way as a horse might
be tamed. Calvin was aware of being called by God, to serve
him in the world. The nature of this vocation was unclear –
but the fact that he was being called seemed beyond dispute.
Grace thus came to designate divine intervention in a situation
of sin and ignorance. It referred to God's ability to turn people
around, to extricate them from the mire of sin, and to tame those
opposed to God – and Calvin included himself and Paul among
the number of those to have experienced grace in this way.

But it came to mean more than being turned inside out.
Although Calvin clearly felt that he had been called by God
(as we have seen, probably at some point in 1533 or 1534),
it was not clear in what capacity or at what location he was
meant to be serving. He had been called – but to what? He
busied himself with various matters, including the writing of a

book, later to become one of the most important publications of the sixteenth century – the *Institutes of the Christian Religion*, published in March 1536. But it was still not clear to him how his calling to be a Christian would work itself out.

Finally, in July 1536 he decided to set out for Strasbourg, and get on with some serious academic studies. A war made the usual route from Paris to Strasbourg impassable. He decided to take another route, by-passing the war by heading further south. He had to pause for a night in a city. That city was Geneva, then in the process of adopting the principles of the Reformation. He was recognised, and asked to stay. Guillaume Farel and Pierre Viret (the reformers who had guided Geneva thus far in its road to reformation) had basically one thing to say to Calvin: you are needed here! As he later related, in his *Reply to Sadoleto*, he had no doubt that he was being called to stay and serve in Geneva. As his later correspondence makes clear, Calvin's sense of vocation was deeply linked with Geneva. When he was temporarily expelled from the city in 1538, he went through a spiritual crisis, apparently believing for a while that his vocation had been cancelled.

In part, this was precipitated by some letters from Louis du Tillet, who had reverted to Catholicism after showing some initial interest in Evangelicalism. Du Tillet suggested that Calvin had foolishly confused a human call – the appeal from Farel and Viret – with a divine call. God had not called him, either to be a pastor, or to work in Geneva. His expulsion from the city proved that point beyond doubt.

But that feeling and that exile were temporary. Calvin seemed to have found out where he was meant to be, and regained a strong sense of having been called by God. 'The Lord', Calvin wrote, 'has given me strong reasons to confirm myself in my calling.' Grace was now linked with a sense of guidance, expressed more rigorously in the doctrine of vocation and related doctrines, such as those of election and predestination. Once more, grace is seen as something which expresses itself in real human life – not just human life in general, but the lives of specific individuals.

Grace, then, concerns the creative, empowering and transforming expression of the graciousness of God in the lives of his people. It is a lifeline in a raging sea of sin and despair. It expresses itself in the forgiveness of sins, the transformation of human weakness, and the guidance of individuals towards their callings in the world. When Paul wrote 'by the grace of God, I am what I am' (1 Corinthians 15:10), he was bearing witness both to God's favour towards him and to the actualisation of that favour in his life. Grace is no abstract idea! To talk about grace virtually amounts to writing biographies – or even autobiographies – as it is to chronicle the gracious acts of God in the lives of men and women in history. Grace is what God does for people. That is an insight which we can use today.

The Reality of Sin – Personal and Structural

Grace is only fully and properly understood when the reality and power of sin have been addressed. The reformers generally had no qualms over speaking about sin. Perhaps two reasons may be given for this observation. First, and not least, the writers of the Reformation believed that they had the means to deal with sin. The doctrine of justification by faith addressed sin head-on, offering peace with God in place of the wrath of God, eternal life in the place of death as the wages of sin, and forgiveness in place of the guilt of sin. This confidence in the reality of justification allowed a degree of assurance in facing up to the reality of sin. Christ died for *real* sins. Perhaps the most powerful – and controversial! – statement of this belief may be found in a letter of Luther to Melanchthon, in which (irritated at the latter's fastidiousness in relation to his personal life), he declared: 'Be a sinner, and sin boldly! But believe in Christ, and rejoice more boldly still!' Luther's point (although probably hopelessly overstated) is that there was no point in becoming obsessed with petty sins: Christ died for the big sins of life, and for that we should rejoice.

But the second reason is perhaps the more significant. The major reformers were not academics, whose experience of life was restricted to the ivory towers of academia. They were pastors, with experience of the profound impact of sin upon human life. They were involved in power struggles within the cities and citadels of Europe, which brought home to them the reality of structural sin. In short, they lived in worlds which made it inevitable that they should realise the impact of sin upon individuals, social structures and communities. They inhabited no Walter Mitty world, but were obliged to face up to the grim realities of human existence.

In part, the reformers themselves bore painful witness to the personal and corporate aspects of sin. Luther found himself placed in a very difficult position during the Peasants' War of 1525. Should he support the peasants' revolt against their oppressive masters – or should he support the princes, upon whose patronage his reformation depended? Caught up in a complex web of possibilities, none of which could easily be described as 'right' or 'wrong', Luther found himself supporting the princes. For many, he compromised himself fatally. Luther's actions, as much as his doctrine of justification, bore witness to his sinful nature. He was forced to recognise the deep roots which sin had made, not only into his personal life, but into every level of human life, individual and corporate.

The contrast with much modern theology is significant, and reflects the shift, noted earlier (p. 31), away from the Reformation paradigm of the theologian as one who is seen to be *within* the community of faith to one who is seen as somehow being *above* that community. Many modern academic theologians have become detached from pastoral work, and have minimal involvement in the affairs of the world. A gap has opened up between academic theorists and the world they are meant to be interpreting and addressing. It is perhaps for reasons such as these that it is the pastors and writers of the Third World who have brought home to the modern period the reality of human sin. Western universities are seen to be just as tainted by sin as the societies within which they are based, or the individuals who teach within them.

In the twentieth century, H. Richard Niebuhr spoke powerfully of a pseudo-gospel in which 'a God without wrath brought people without sin into a kingdom without judgement through the ministrations of a Christ without a cross'. For much liberal theology, the notion of sin is to be dismissed as outdated and irrelevant, not least because it poses a powerful challenge to the notion of fundamental human goodness, upon which so much liberal optimism rests. To rediscover Reformation spirituality is to return to an age when the reality of sin was freely acknowledged. Sin has assumed for many liberal writers much the same status as sex among the Victorians: it was something that other people did, and which you didn't talk about anyway. The more open and healthy attitude of the reformers has much to commend it. It also encourages a degree of openness in relation to a difficult area of spirituality – the persistence of sin among believers.

Sinful Christians – A Contradiction in Terms?

Most Christians are aware of a sense of sin; indeed, very often it is the most mature Christians that are most aware of their sin. But underlying this practical observation is a theoretical difficulty. How can sin and faith coexist? How can Christians, who are meant to be righteous, also be sinners? Psychology and theology need to inter-relate on this issue. Luther's discussion of precisely this point is one of the most helpful aspects of his spirituality. He deals with the question in the Romans lectures of 1515–16, and we shall examine what he has to say on the matter.

Luther draws a basic distinction between the way we are regarded by God, and the way we regard ourselves. There is a fundamental difference between our status in our own eyes, and in the sight of God. Luther uses the terms 'intrinsic' and 'extrinsic' in this connection. Having thus clarified this distinction between the internal human and external divine perspectives, Luther considers the difference between believers and unbelievers (to use his terms, saints and hypocrites). 'The saints are always sinners in their own sight, and therefore are always justified extrinsically; the hypocrites, however, are always righteous in their own sight, and are therefore always sinners extrinsically.' Believers thus regard themselves as sinners; but in the sight of God, they are righteous on account of their justification. God reckons believers to be righteous, on account of their faith. Through faith, the believer is clothed with the righteousness of Christ, in much the same way, Luther suggests, as Ezekiel 16:8 speaks of God covering our nakedness with his garment. For Luther, faith is the right (or righteous) relationship to God. Sin and righteousness thus co-exist; we remain sinners inwardly, but are righteous extrinsically, in the sight of God. By confessing our sins in faith, we stand in a right and righteous relationship with God. From our own perspective we are sinners; but in the perspective of God, we are righteous.

> Now the saints are always aware of their sin and seek right-eousness from God in accordance with his mercy. And for this very reason, they are regarded as righteous by God. Thus in their own eyes (and in reality!) they are sinners – but in the eyes of God they are righteous, because he reckons them as such on account of their confession of their sin. In reality they are sinners; but they are righteous by the imputation of a merciful God. They are unknowingly righteous, and knowingly sinners. They are sinners in fact, but righteous in hope.

Luther is not necessarily implying that this co-existence of sin and righteousness is a permanent condition. His point is that God shields our sin through his righteousness. His righteousness is like a protective covering, under which we may battle with our sin. But – and this is Luther's central insight – the existence of sin does not negate our status as Christians. In justification, we are given the status of righteousness, while we work with God towards attaining the nature of righteousness. In that God has promised to make us righteous one day, finally eliminating our sin, there is a sense in which we are already righteous in his sight. Luther makes this point as follows:

> It is just like someone who is sick, and who believes the doctor who promises his full recovery. In the meantime, he obeys the doctor's orders in the hope of the promised recovery, and abstains from those things which he has been told to lay off, so that he may in no way hinder the promised return to health . . . Now is this sick man well? In fact, he is both sick and

well at the same time. He is sick in reality – but he is well on account of the sure promise of the doctor, whom he trusts, and who reckons him as already being cured.

Obviously enjoying this medical analogy, Luther takes it a stage further. Having established that illness is an analogue of sin, and health of righteousness, he concludes:

So he is at one and the same time both a sinner and righteous. He is a sinner in reality, but righteous by the sure imputation and promise of God that he will continue to deliver him from sin until he has completely cured him. So he is entirely healthy in hope, but a sinner in reality.

This approach is helpful, in that it accounts for the persistence of sin in believers, while at the same time accounting for the gradual transformation of the believer and the future elimination of that sin. But it is not necessary to be perfectly righteous to be a Christian! Sin does not point to unbelief, or to a failure on the part of God; rather, it points to the continued need to entrust one's person to the gentle care of God.

The pastoral importance of this way of thinking is considerable. A colleague once told me of a meeting which he had recently attended at his local church, dealing with the theme of 'self-esteem'. Everyone was asked to rate themselves on a scale between zero (terrible) and ten (perfect). Most of those people – being modest Americans – rated themselves between four and six (not especially good, but not especially bad either). The visiting speaker (who had been reading some fashionable works of psychotherapy) then declared that they all ought to rate themselves as ten; they were, he said, all perfect, and merely suffered from a complete lack of self-esteem. This provoked an amused reaction among those present, who generally regarded their self-estimation as entirely accurate, and that of their visiting speaker as totally deluded.

This incident brings out neatly the reluctance on the part of many modern persons to accept the fact that they are less than perfect. To concede imperfection seems tantamount to a humiliating and degrading admission of total failure. This denial of sin finds its natural expression in the myth of perfection – the totally unrealistic assertion that the way we are is the way we are meant to be. The doctrine of justification invites us to acknowledge our imperfection and sin – while rejoicing in the purpose and power of God to transform the poverty of our nature into the likeness of Jesus Christ. Augustine once likened the church to a hospital. It is a community of sick people, united by their willingness to acknowledge their sin and their hope and trust in the skill of the physicians to whose care they are committed. Luther, as we have seen above, continues this way of thinking: we may be sinful in reality, but we are righteous in hope.

The story also illustrates how important, helpful and *Christian* Luther's approach to this problem of self-esteem turns out to be. God accepts us as we are. You do not have to rate yourself as ten to be a Christian. Nor is perfection a prerequisite of acceptance in the sight of God. God accepts you just as you are – he grants you the status of ten, on account of his promise to renew and refashion you totally. You score four, five or six – but you are accepted nonetheless. In his graciousness, God accepts you. You don't have to delude yourself (or think that God is deluded) by pretending that you are perfect. The justification of sinners rests upon no delusions, no legal fictions, and no pretence of holiness. God accepts us for what we are, while he works within us that which he wants us to be. We are given the *status* of ten, in the light of God's promise to rebuild us, and finally to give us the *nature* of ten. And that gives us encouragement and motivation to move up the scale, working on our weaknesses and shortcomings. And so, by the grace of God, our fours, fives or sixes become eight, nine or ten. God grants to us now a status which reflects his vision, intention and promise concerning what we shall be, when recreated by his grace.

But now consider the approach of our amateur psycho-therapist. He was telling his hearers that they were perfect. That was regarded as ludicrous by those who listened to him, for two reasons. First, it did not accord with their experience. They knew themselves to be less than perfect. Whatever pretence of perfection they may have chosen to maintain in public, in private they were perfectly aware of their sin. And second, it removed any motivation for self-improvement. If you score ten out of ten, there is nothing more to be achieved. The scene is set for quietism, a total indifference to self-improvement and growth in holiness. Luther's approach avoids both these pitfalls. It declares that we *are* sinners (which resonates with our own experience and knowledge of ourselves), and that there is considerable room for improvement – but it also affirms that we are still able to have the status of being righteous in the sight of God. The twentieth-century German-American writer Paul Tillich captured this insight when he wrote: 'We must accept that we have been accepted, despite being unacceptable.'

An awareness of sin, then, is not necessarily a symptom of some kind of lapse from faith, or a sign of an imperfect commitment to God. It can be nothing more than a reflection of the continuing struggle against sin, which is an essential component of the process of justification and renewal. Let Luther have the final word on this point. 'In ourselves, we are sinners, and yet through faith we are righteous by the imputation of God. For we trust him who promises to deliver us, and in the meantime struggle so that sin may not overwhelm us, but that we may stand up to it until he finally takes it away from us.'

The Sacraments: Reminders of Grace

'Let my people grow!' has been the watchword of the church growth movement of the late twentieth century. In its initial phase, the Reformation had to grow, if it was to survive. Yet mere growth in numbers was not seen as adequate to the needs of the new Evangelical communities throughout Europe. Numerical increase within the churches of the Reformation had to be matched by a growth in faith, discernment and commitment on the part of their members – otherwise the end result would be large groups of superficial Christians, incapable of sustaining their faith.

Spiritual growth was thus seen as a central area of concern. Resources had to be deployed and techniques developed for the nurture of faith. In this closing section, we shall consider one of the means by which the reformers attempted to deepen the quality of faith of their people, in the belief that they remain of relevance today. The sacraments were seen as visible signs and reminders of the grace of God – a powerful aid to meditation, possessing the potential to lead on to new qualities of Christian faith and understanding.

The Reformation was born in controversy. Controversy can be helpful, in that it stimulates exploration and clarification. The fundamental impulse which the controversies of the fourth century gave to the development of Christian thinking concerning the divinity of Jesus Christ and the nature of the Trinity are a witness to this point. But controversy can also have a profoundly negative effect. In the heat of a debate, with so much resting upon the outcome, parties are prone to exaggerate and to posture. As a result, ideas and practices which at other times would have been perfectly acceptable are rejected out of hand. The characteristic Protestant devaluation of the sacraments is a case in point. Protestants, perhaps fearing that an affirmative attitude to the sacraments might be construed as a dangerous concession to their Catholic opponents, have tended to treat the sacraments with considerably less appreciation than they deserve.

For example, in Victorian England it became routine for Anglican Evangelicals to be low churchmen (having no place for the institution of the church in their theology or spirituality), and hostile to any form of worship which gave any position of importance to the sacraments. Such was the religious polarisation at the time that word and sacrament were virtually seen as mutually exclusive. The result has been an impoverishment of the Protestant spiritual tradition. Happily, the study of the spirituality of the first period of the Reformation allows us to see how this situation can be remedied. If any aspect of the Reformation heritage needs to be reclaimed and renewed by modern Evangelicalism, it is in the field of the sacraments.

A theme central to the Reformation emphasis upon the importance of the sacraments to an Evangelical spirituality is that of *divine accommodation to human weakness*. The idea is especially associated with Calvin, who is usually regarded as its most lucid expositor. Calvin argues as follows. All good speakers know and understand the limitations of their audiences. And they adapt their way of speaking accordingly. They modify their language to suit the needs and abilities of their listeners, avoiding difficult words and ideas, and using more appropriate ways of speaking in their place. This 'principle of accommodation' also extends to the use of analogies and visual aids. Many people find ideas and concepts difficult to handle, forcing responsible public speakers to use stories and illustrations to make their point.

So it is with God, Calvin argues. He accommodates himself to our weakness. He comes down to our level, using powerful images and ways of speaking which enable him to reveal himself to a wide range of individual abilities. No one is excluded from learning about God on account of their educational achievement. That God can use such lowly ways of revealing himself does not reflect any weakness or shortcoming on *his* part; it reflects a weakness on *our* part, which God graciously acknowledges and deals with. God is able to deploy a wide range of resources in creating and sustaining faith – words, concepts, analogies, models, signs and symbols. The sacraments are to be seen as an important element in this arsenal of resources.

For the first generation of reformers, the sacraments were God's response to human weakness. Knowing our difficulty in receiving and responding to his promises, God supplemented his word with visible and tangible signs of his gracious favour. They are an accommodation to our abilities. The sacraments represent the promises of God, mediated through objects of the everyday world. In his *Propositions on the Mass* (1521), Melanchthon stressed that sacraments were primarily a gracious divine accommodation to human weakness. In a series of sixty-five propositions, Melanchthon put forward what he regarded as a reliable and responsible approach to the place of the sacraments in Christian spirituality. 'Signs are the means by which we may be both reminded and reassured of the word of faith.' Not every sign is a sacrament; a sacrament is an *instituted and authorised* sign of grace, the credentials of which rest upon a firm Evangelical foundation. They are not signs of our own choosing; they have been chosen for us.

In an ideal world, Melanchthon suggests, human beings would be prepared to trust God on the basis of his word alone. However, one of the weaknesses of fallen human nature is its need for signs (Melanchthon appeals to the story of Gideon as he makes this point). For Melanchthon, sacraments are signs: 'What some call sacraments, we call signs – or, if you prefer, sacramental signs.' These sacramental signs enhance our trust in God. 'In order to mitigate this distrust in the human heart, God has added signs to the word.' Sacraments are thus signs of the grace of God, added to the promises of grace in order to reassure and strengthen the faith of fallen human beings.

Luther made a similar point, defining sacraments as 'promises with signs attached to them' or 'divinely instituted signs and the promise of forgiveness of sins.' Interestingly, Luther uses the term 'pledge' (*Pfand*) to emphasise the security-giving character of the eucharist. The bread and the wine reassure us of the reality of the divine promise of forgiveness, making it easier for us to accept it, and having accepted it, to hold it firmly.

> In order that we might be certain of this promise of Christ, and truly rely on it without any doubt, he has given us the most precious and costly seal and pledge – his true body and blood, given under the bread and wine. These are the very same as those with which he obtained for us the gift and the promise of this precious and gracious treasure, surrendering his life in order that we might receive and accept the promised grace.

The bread and wine of the communion service thus simultaneously remind us of the *reality* and the *cost* of the grace of God on the one hand, and of our response to this grace in faith.

God's promises are thus both real and costly. The death of Christ is a token of both the trustworthiness and the enormous price of the grace of God. Luther develops this point by using the idea of a 'testament', understood in the sense of a 'last will and testament'.

> Christ declares that this is the new testament in his blood, poured out for us (Luke 22:20) . . . Everyone knows that a testament is a promise made by someone who is about to

die, in which he names his bequest and appoints his heirs. So a testament involves, in the first place, the death of the testator, and in the second, the promise of an inheritance and the naming of an heir.

Luther's insight here is this. A testament involves promises which become operational only after the death of the person who made those promises in the first place. The communion service thus makes three vitally important points:

1. It affirms the promises of grace and forgiveness.
2. It identifies those to whom those promises are made.
3. It declares the death of the one who made those promises.

Thus it dramatically proclaims that the promises of grace and forgiveness are now in effect. It is 'a promise of the forgiveness of sins made to us by God, and such a promise as has been confirmed by the death of the son of God'. By proclaiming the death of Christ, the community of faith affirms that the precious promises of forgiveness and eternal life are now effective for those with faith.

But how can such mean and common things as water, bread or wine come to have such importance for the Christian life? Surely this represents an unjustified lapse into some kind of nature religion or misguided materialism? Surely the whole point of Christianity is to direct our attention away from material objects, towards the greater reality of God himself? Why bother with material objects, when we have the word of God at our disposal? Luther deals with this important question as follows:

In the sacraments we see nothing wonderful – just ordinary water, bread and wine, and the words of a preacher. There is nothing spectacular about that. But we must learn to discover what a glorious majesty lies hidden beneath these despised things. It is precisely the same with Christ in the incarnation. We see a frail, weak and mortal human being – yet he is nothing other than the majesty of God himself. In precisely the same way, God himself speaks to us and deals with us in these ordinary and despised materials.

Luther's Christology informs his approach to the sacraments. God is able to make himself known through the things of this world. But, as Luther and his colleagues stressed, we are only *authorised* to treat certain physical signs as sacraments.

Perhaps a personal illustration will bring out the point which Luther has in mind. When I was a research student at Cambridge University, I used regularly to visit an elderly man who lived in a nearby village. One spring, we got round to talking about the daffodils which grew in profusion near his home. 'I like daffodils,' he told me. 'New life after the winter. They remind me of the resurrection.' He died that summer. And ever since, I have found that the sight of spring daffodils reminds me both of the resurrection and of that old man.

But that memory and association is purely personal. The community of faith cannot become a slave to the personal associations of its members. The sacraments are about certain quite definite things having associations for *all* the members of the community of faith – associations and memories which are reinforced and deepened by their use in Christian worship. But how, it might be asked, can such mundane things as bread or wine come to have such powerful associations? Zwingli gave a helpful answer to this question. (Nowadays, we would refer to his approach as 'a theory of transsignification'. Happily, Zwingli uses no such term! One of the delights of the writings of the Reformation is their pastoral tone and their everyday language – something of a relief to anyone who has been worn out by the technicality of what passes as theology today.)

Perhaps we should begin our discussion one step further back. For Zwingli, one of the central purposes of the eucharist is to remind us of Christ. He gives an analogy to make this point. Think of a merchant, about to set off on a long business trip (Zwingli probably has in mind the business men of his native Zurich, who had forged important trading links with Italy and Germany). Before he leaves, he gives his wife a ring, containing a small portrait of himself. That ring, Zwingli tells us, is a reminder of the husband's love for his wife, and of his promise to return. In his absence, she can recall his memory. The ring is *his*, and thus possesses strongly personal associations. She links it in her memory with the day her husband left, and associates it with his promise to return. While he is away, the ring is a link with her husband.

Zwingli suggests that the bread and the wine have similar associations for believers. They are linked in their minds with the Last Supper, when Christ prepared to depart from this world and this life. They are a reminder of his promise to return. And, in the absence of Christ, his people may continue to cherish the bread and the wine as pledges and reminders of their Lord. The bread and the wine become special. But how? What *is* special about the bread and the wine in a communion service? How do they differ from ordinary bread and wine?

Zwingli answers this question with two analogies. Consider a ring, he suggests, in two quite different contexts. In the first context, the ring is merely present. Perhaps you can imagine a ring lying on a table, or in a display tray in a jeweller's window. It is a piece of precious metal – but there is not much more that could be said about it. *It has no associations.* Now imagine that ring transferred to a new context. It is placed on the finger of a king. It now has personal associations, deriving from its connection with him – such as his authority, power and majesty. These associations arise through transfer from the original context to the new context: the ring itself remains completely unchanged.

Changing his images, Zwingli suggests we think of some lilies growing in a field. Now imagine them transferred to a completely different context – a bridal gown. The lilies, now woven into the shape and form of a crown, take on a completely new meaning. They are part of the bridal celebrations. On account of their connection with the bride on her marriage day, they take on associations of rejoicing and celebration – associations which were quite absent in their native state. Once more, a change of context leads to a change in associations.

In each case, the same pattern emerges: the object is unchanged in itself, while its signification alters dramatically. The signification – in other words, the associations of the object – can change, without any difference in the nature of the object itself. Zwingli suggests that exactly the same process can be seen with the bread and the wine. In their ordinary everyday context, they are plain bread and wine, with no especial associations. But when they are moved into a new context, they take on new and important associations. When they are placed at the centre of a worshipping community, and when the story of the last night of the life of Christ on earth is retold, they become powerful reminders of the foundational events of the Christian faith. It is their context which gives them this meaning; they remain unchanged in themselves. Many individuals find this approach helpful – not least because it avoids complex metaphysical questions (such as those lurking behind the medieval idea of transubstantiation, according to which the communion bread actually became the body of Christ).

The Reformation stress upon the need for faith, and the high priority given to the word of God, are thus not inconsistent with giving a place of importance to the sacraments in Christian spirituality. Indeed, they are entirely in line with both these emphases. In the first place, the sacraments are intended to support faith; without faith, they are utterly devoid of value. Luther makes this point with characteristic force:

> Just think of how many people there are who like to be certain about the Christian faith, or who hanker after a sign from heaven telling them how they stand in relation to God, and whether they are among the elect! But what use would such a sign be if they still do not have faith? What good are signs without faith? What use are the venerable signs of the sacraments (or the very words of God himself, for that matter) in our own day and age, if they are not received with faith?

The sacraments gain their effectiveness within a context of faith.

In the second place, the sacraments are intended to confirm the word of God, not act as a substitute for it. As Luther wrote, 'If you leave out the word of God, baptism becomes nothing but water, and the Lord's Supper nothing but bread.' The sacraments link together word and sign, the promise of grace and a physical pointer to this grace. 'The most important part of the sacraments is the word and the covenant of God. Without these, the sacraments are dead and useless.' They are an accommodation to our weakness, as God attempts to make his promises more real to us.

Understood in this way, the sacraments – especially the eucharist – have a real and important function within Reformation spirituality. They are God-given and God-authorised signs of grace, designed to deepen our trust in him. They have the potential to remind us of our Christian roots, and to evoke the powerful memory of the death of Christ for our salvation. Rightly understood, they have enormous potential as spiritual resources. It is true that, as a matter of history, Protestant churches have played down their importance. But this de-emphasis of the sacraments is linked with the great religious controversies of the post-Reformation period, including the Wars of Religion and the Thirty Years War. Those are now firmly behind us. Perhaps the time has come to reclaim the sacraments within Protestant spirituality.

Much the same comment might be made in relation to the idea of spiritual discipline, to which we may now turn.

9   Discipline and Freedom: Justification by Faith and the Christian Life

One of the central insights of the Reformation is its doctrine of justification by faith – or, more accurately, justification by grace through faith. Indeed, this doctrine, which we shall consider in more detail in this chapter, is generally regarded as lying at the heart of the Reformation struggle for a return to authentic forms of Christian doctrine and spirituality. For the reformers, the whole of Christian existence, from its beginning to its end, was a result of and an expression of the grace of God – a fact which shapes the entire Christian outlook upon life.

The Reformation emphasis upon the graciousness of God restored a vital perspective to Christian spirituality. Salvation is a gracious gift, not something to be earned. Our status in the sight of God is something granted to us, not something we attain through our merits or achievements. We are like beggars, dependent upon the grace of God – not like litigants, suing God for whatever we can get from him. For Luther, the gospel of grace liberates us from an oppressive mentality of achievement – the mind-set that insists that we must do God some favours before he will take any notice of us.

This new stress upon the grace of God came like a breath of fresh air in the midst of the stifling world of much popular late-medieval spirituality. Yet, in its wake, this rediscovery of grace brought the possibility of a serious misunderstanding: the suggestion that the graciousness of God abolishes any need for human discipline. Christian freedom might be thought to do away with any sense of Christian obligation.

Although these ideas did indeed gain credibility in some sections of the Reformation, the mainline reformers believed them to be seriously inconsistent with the gospel. It was necessary to address the question of the relation of freedom and responsibility within the Christian life. In his *Freedom of a Christian* (1520), Luther stated this relationship in terms of two propositions:

> A Christian is a perfectly free lord of all, subject to nobody.
> A Christian is a perfectly dutiful servant of all, subject to everyone.

This concluding chapter aims to explore the doctrine of justification by faith in some depth, and discover its relevance for spirituality. Although we have already touched upon some of its many facets in the previous chapter, many remain to be uncovered.

Justification by Faith and Human Achievement

One of the central affirmations of the doctrine of justification by faith is that God gives us all that is necessary for salvation. We do not have to achieve salvation; we do not have to earn salvation; it is something which is offered to us, and which we are invited merely to receive. It is, however, a transforming gift. To accept our justification is to open the way to the transformation of our existence. In justification, we are given the status of being righteous in the sight of God while, at the same time, the process of conforming us to God in Christ begins. Our God-given change in status is accompanied by a God-wrought change in our hearts. The external gift of righteousness is complemented with the internal work of renewal of the Holy Spirit.

Before exploring the implications of this, we must look at a few difficulties people experience in dealing with the spiritual implications of justification by faith. The first difficulty concerns the term 'justification' itself, which seems unfamiliar to modern ears. 'Justification' is most commonly understood in the modern period as a defence of one's position in an argument or legal case, or, for writers, the process of making right-hand margins uniform across a printed page. So how can a term most familiar from the world of word processing have any real relevance for Christian spirituality?

The English word 'justification' is an attempt to denote the Old Testament idea of being 'right before God'. Through a contorted and complex tradition of translation and interpretation – from Hebrew to Greek, from Greek to Latin, and finally from Latin to English – 'justification' has come to refer to the status of being righteous in the sight of God. To be justified is to be right with God. For Luther, as we noted earlier, to have faith is to be right with God – that is, to live in an attitude of trust in God. Faith is the right way to live, in the sight of God. It may therefore be helpful if the word 'justification' is paraphrased, perhaps to give 'being right with God'. Similarly, 'to be justified' could be paraphrased as 'to be put in a right relationship with God'.

However, this is not a problem unique to Christian theology: all technical words need to be explained to their audiences. The American phrase 'the fifth amendment to the constitution' may seem technical and unfamiliar to many – but it still refers to something of vital importance. C.S. Lewis once wrote:

> We must learn the language of our audience. And let me say at the outset that it is no use laying down *a priori* what the 'plain man' does or does not understand. You have to find out by experience . . . You must translate every bit of your theology into the vernacular. This is very troublesome . . . but it is essential. It is also of the greatest service to your own thought. I have come to the conclusion that if you cannot translate your own thoughts into uneducated language, then your thoughts are confused. Power to translate is the test of having really understood your own meaning.

If the doctrine of justification by faith is 'unintelligible', it is because we have made it so, and have failed to *explain* its power and relevance for the human situation. The failure lies with us, and not with the doctrine.

Second, the phrase 'justification by faith' is open to a serious misunderstanding. It might appear to have the following sense: an individual is justified *on account of faith*. In other words, the human activity of faith is the basis of God's decision to grant us the status of being righteous in his sight. If this were the case, this would amount to a doctrine of justification by works, with faith merely being seen as a special type of good work.

In fact, the phrase 'justification by faith' has a quite different meaning, which is perhaps best understood by considering a Latin phrase Melanchthon uses in explaining it. We are justified *propter Christum per fidem* – that is, on account of Christ, through faith. The basis of God's decision to place us in a right relationship with him lies in Jesus Christ himself. We are justified on account of his obedience during his lifetime, and his death upon the cross. It is because of him, and not because of anything we have done or will do, that we are made right with God. But the means by which we are justified is faith. Faith is like a channel, through which the benefits of Christ flow to us. Or, to use an image of Luther's which we considered in an earlier chapter, faith is like a marriage bond, which unites us to Christ (see pp. 100–2). We are not justified *on account of faith*; we are justified *through* faith. It is the work of Christ, not our faith, which is the foundation of justification. Faith is the means by which the work of Christ is applied to our lives. This is no doctrine of justification on account of human achievement; it is a doctrine of justification on account of Christ.

But the doctrine implies still more than this. Faith is itself a gift of God. In other words, both the external foundation and the internal means of appropriation of justification are God-given. Faith is not something which we can achieve; it is something achieved within us by God. This assertion might seem bewildering, if faith is simply understood as 'assent to the existence of God', or 'belief in the key doctrines of Christianity'. However, as we noted in an earlier chapter, the Reformation understanding of faith embraces far more than this. Faith unites us to Christ and all his benefits. Everything necessary for salvation has been done, and done well, by God. The central Reformation doctrine of the assurance of faith rests upon this recognition.

This naturally leads to the third difficulty. The doctrine of justification by faith, as expounded above, sounds as if it has no fundamental concern with morality or obedience. No reference to good works, or the need to live out a good Christian life, has been made. So important is this point that we shall consider it further in the following section; however, some initial comments may be of use at this stage.

The fundamental concern of the reformers was to avoid the suggestion that we are justified on account of something which we achieve. This was seen as having three unacceptable consequences:

1. It placed God under an obligation to reward our actions, thus denying the *graciousness* of justification and the freedom of God.

2. It treated human works as being meritorious, capable of having a purchase upon justification. Justification would thus have become a reward, something given to us on the basis of human merit. The reformers believed that this was dangerously presumptive.

3. It encouraged a spirituality of achievement, by which humans were encouraged to believe that they could achieve unaided the necessary standards for justification.

Each of these dangers had been noted within medieval Catholic theology; nevertheless, the strategies adopted in relation to them were complex and confusing, involving fine theological distinctions (such as that between congruous and condign merit) which ordinary people found – and still find – difficult to understand. It must be remembered that theology was something virtually totally restricted to the monasteries. Monks, familiar with the complex distinctions of scholastic theology, could perhaps cope with these ideas; ordinary people must have found them baffling, and thoroughly unhelpful. The reformers believed that the only way to avoid a religion of merits was to stress the total gratuity of justification. God justifies us without any reference to our achievements – past, present or future.

The origins of the Christian life thus owe nothing to our moral or spiritual achievements. But once the Christian life has begun, a new and important role is given to human works. On account of the transformative nature of faith, our natures are altered, so that we naturally want to perform good works. Faith is pregnant with good works, as the writings of the later Reformation would have it. The Christian life is *begun* without any contribution from us; it continues through good works, as we are renewed and regenerated by the Holy Spirit, and give expression both to our thankfulness to God and to the reality of our new natures, by moral living. The essential insight here is that human works are a *response to* justification, not a *precondition for* justification. We shall explore these ideas again presently in greater detail.

So what are the implications for Christian spirituality of this central doctrine of the Reformation? Perhaps the most important implication concerns the phenomenon of the self-made person, especially as it centres upon a religion of effort. Modern western society, especially in the United States of America, is very achievement-orientated. 'You are what you make of yourself' is a key slogan of the enterprise culture. 'You have to lift yourself up by your own bootlaces.' Many are deeply influenced by the secular values of success instilled into us by our families and peers. And these secular attitudes have important spiritual spin-offs. Many feel that they must *do* something or *achieve* something before God can love them. The gospel proclamation of the *unconditionality* of God's love for us can be difficult for such people to accept – because it so obviously contradicts the standards of western culture.

Surely we must do something before God can accept us? Many are taught that dependency on others is to be discouraged. As a result, they believe strongly in the cult of independence: personal fulfilment is based on not being dependent on anyone or anything. The idea that God loves us, however, is an invitation to learn to depend on God. This clashes with the set of values many have absorbed unconsciously from secular culture, which asserts that the way to get ahead in the world is through being independent.

Interestingly, similar attitudes can be instanced from late medieval spirituality, with its stress upon human works and effort. Luther mounts a powerful challenge to these attitudes.

We are asked to accept that we have been accepted by God through Jesus Christ, despite being unacceptable. This, Luther suggests, is difficult for human pride to bear. 'The only thing that resists this idea of justification is the pride of the human heart, which is proud through its unbelief.' Our status before God is something given, not something earned. 'Sinners are attractive because they are loved; they are not loved because they are attractive.' God's love for us is not dependent upon our achievements. We can never earn our salvation. We do not need to be high achievers to become Christians; it is God, not us, who achieves things.

Luther died in the early hours of Thursday, 17 February 1546. His last word was '*Ja* – Yes', muttered as he lay dying, in response to one of his friends, who asked if he was 'willing to persevere in the Christian faith and doctrine that you have preached'. Shortly after his death, his friends found a note lying on a table in the same house. It was Luther's final written statement. Its last six words read: '*Wir sind Bettler. Hoc est verum*' – 'We are beggars. This is true'. For Luther, Christians are spiritual beggars, incapable of achieving anything unaided, and dependent totally upon the generosity of a God who gives. Luther's entire spirituality could be summed up in those final six words. God gives; we receive – gladly and gratefully.

Grace and Discipline

It is perhaps one of the greatest paradoxes of the sixteenth century that a movement which placed enormous emphasis upon divine grace should also give considerable weight to human discipline. Surely there is a contradiction here? Is not the very idea of personal and corporate discipline inconsistent with an emphasis upon the priority of the grace of God?

At first sight, the case for inconsistency seems impressive. The doctrine of justification by faith is profoundly liberating, in that it cuts the ground from under any religion of achievement. The idea that it is God who achieves things – not us! – is excellent news, especially for those who are aware of their fragility and weakness, or who lack confidence in their own abilities. To speak of the importance of discipline in the Christian life thus seems to run counter to this liberating theme. Is it not a lapse into the mind-set of medieval monasticism, with its emphasis upon regulation of life?

But, on closer inspection, the suspected contradiction disappears. The answer to this apparent inconsistency lies in the transformative dimensions of divine grace. Grace does not leave us where we are – it moves us on. Luther's image of a physician, noted above, is helpful here: grace does not merely diagnose our situation; it heals it. It does not merely point out our weakness; it comes to our aid. The human nature that was incapable of justifying itself, on account of its inability to perform good works or to achieve anything of significance, is radically transformed. With the aid of grace, it becomes capable of doing things – for God and with God.

Let us begin our analysis of this question by considering the relation between faith and good works. Two theological models are provided by the reformers to enable us to make sense of this situation. The first is due to Luther. Drawing upon the New Testament imagery of a tree, Luther argues that the productivity of the tree is totally dependent upon its roots. A good root leads to good fruit. Faith, Luther argues, provides the sound root which is essential to the life of the tree. From that point onwards, it is able to produce good fruit naturally. The presence of a good root establishes the final link in a complex biological process which, by the laws of nature, leads to the production of fruit. The tree does not need to be told to produce that fruit – it just happens naturally. Once the root is established, enabling the tree to draw upon nourishment from the ground, the remainder of the process takes care of itself.

So it is with faith, Luther argues. Faith is like that good root. Once it is established, a process is begun which naturally leads to the living out of a good life and the performance of good works. A true faith naturally leads to good works.

From faith flows love and joy in the Lord, and from love a joyful, willing and free mind that serves our neighbours willingly . . . As our heavenly Father has freely come to our assistance in

Christ, so we also ought to help our neighbours through our bodies and our works, and each should become, as it were, a Christ to others.

Yet just as a tree cannot bear fruit until its root has been established, so no good works are possible before faith. Luther here draws upon an important distinction, going back to Augustine of Hippo, between morally good works, and works which are done as a consequence of faith in God. For Luther, the essence of good works is that they are performed in a spirit of thankfulness and a desire to please God. Faith thus establishes the proper motivation for good works. They are not an end in themselves; they are not undertaken to impress our friends and neighbours; rather, they are the natural response of the believer to God. 'Our faith in Christ does not free us from works, but from false opinions concerning works (such as the stupid idea that we are justified through works).' We are thus liberated from an oppressive achievement-orientated mind-set.

Calvin develops a somewhat more sophisticated model, drawing upon the notion of the personal presence of Christ within the believer. The gospel, Calvin argues, concerns our encounter with Jesus Christ, and union with him through faith. What we receive from God through faith is not so much a series of gifts, but one supreme gift – the gracious indwelling of Jesus Christ himself. Calvin is here drawing upon Luther's famous analogy of the marriage between Christ and the believer (see p. 101). The believer is incorporated into the life of the risen Christ – and has integrated Christ into the life of faith in an *internal*, rather than a purely *external* manner. Faith unites the believer to Jesus Christ, acting as a channel through which both the person and the benefits of Christ are conveyed. This union with Christ has two main consequences: Calvin, basing himself on 1 Corinthians 6:11, refers to them as the 'double grace' of *justification* and *sanctification*.

Christ 'is made unto us wisdom and righteousness, and sanctification and redemption' (1 Corinthians 1:30). Christ, therefore, does not justify anyone without also sanctifying him or her.

> Those blessings are joined by a permanent and unbreakable tie. Anyone whom he enlightens by his wisdom, he also redeems; anyone whom he redeems, he also justifies; whom he justifies, he also sanctifies.

In that we really have been united with Christ through faith, we really do share in his wisdom and righteousness. In that our redemptive encounter and union with Christ is totally gratuitous, the gratuity of justification is upheld – just as the necessity of regeneration and sanctification is upheld, on account of the unbreakable link between the union with Christ and sanctification. Justification is still treated as the external pronouncement of God that we are right in his sight – but it occurs on the basis of the presence within us of the living Christ. A formidable theological link is thus established between the personal presence of Christ within the believer, and justification.

But for our purposes, the most important feature of this model concerns its rigorous analysis of sanctification – the process of renewal by which the Christian is renewed internally, and conformed to the image of Christ. For Calvin, justification and sanctification are both direct consequences of the presence of Christ within the believer. Justification does not cause sanctification; sanctification does not cause justification; rather, both are caused by the transforming presence of Christ, which makes the believer right in the sight of God (justification), and simultaneously begins the process of conforming the believer to the likeness of Christ (sanctification). Sanctification is not understood as a human work; it is the work of God within us, conforming our likeness to that of Christ, who is already present within us. It is almost as if the presence of Christ in believers acts as a catalyst, by which the process of renewal and refashioning may take place.

Thus both Luther and Calvin lay a theological foundation for a series of vital spiritual insights. We are not justified by our obedience – but justification leads to obedience. A number of Pauline insights from the New Testament are here merged, to yield a consistent and responsible Christian spirituality. Christians are those who are 'in Christ', sharing in his righteousness and sanctification (1 Corinthians 1:30); Christians are those who are being conformed to Christ – including being conformed to his obedience; obedience arises from faith (Romans 1:5). This insight is captured perfectly by the Barmen Declaration (1934), which brought this basic principle of classic Evangelical spirituality to bear upon the situation of the German church under Adolf Hitler:

> As Jesus Christ is God's assurance of the forgiveness of all our sins, so in the same way and with the same seriousness he is also God's mighty claim upon our entire life. Through him there takes place a joyful deliverance from the godless bonds of this world for a free, grateful service to his creatures.

Yet a difficulty arises here. If justifying faith spontaneously leads to good works, what can be said in the case of the person who claims to be a Christian, yet shows no obvious signs of good works? An initial point may be made. The term 'good works' does not necessarily mean 'publicly observable and publicly performed good works'. The individual who has put his or her trust in Christ may express that faith in quiet ways, known only to a few individuals. For Luther in particular, the idea of drawing public attention to one's works or spiritual achievements is repugnant, coming dangerously close to self-glorification. But a genuine point remains to be answered: are works proof of faith? May a faith which does not obviously express itself in good works be regarded as Christian? Can one judge this faith?

This was a point of real concern to the reformers, and we may consider their approach in relation to Calvin's congregation at Geneva. Calvin was convinced that there were many within his congregation who were Christian in name only. But who was he to decide who was a Christian, and who was not? Only God can make such a judgement and such a decision. Basing himself on the parable of the Wheat and the Tares (Matthew 13:24–30), Calvin argued that his job was to preach the gospel faithfully and patiently, declaring the wonders of the gospel, and making its implications for human actions as clear as possible. But he could not, and should not, judge who was a Christian and who was not. The separation of believer and non-believer was best left to God. As the parable suggested, any pre-emptive attempt to separate them within the congregation could lead to damage. We cannot afford to be judgemental in this matter, as it requires access to the hidden motives of the human heart. But, as Calvin stressed, the preacher and pastor may expound the gospel and its consequences as clearly as possible, and leave the rest up to God. The pastor must stress that the gospel should lead to good works – but leave any judgement concerning the faith of his or her people up to God.

The scene is thus set for the final component of this analysis – the importance of discipline in the Christian life. This is very often misunderstood as a degeneration into some kind of legalism – an observance of restrictive and oppressive regulations, just for the sake of it. This is not an adequate representation of the situation. Discipline is a response to and a result of faith, not something independent of faith. No one is suggesting for one moment that you can get into the kingdom of God by observing a set of rules or regulations!

Think of discipline as a response of the whole person to God – including bringing your life into line with his will. This means working at those areas in which you still fall far short of what you know to be his will for you. Discipline is about deepening your commitment to God in every aspect of your life. It is not about the mindless observance of rules; it is about developing strategies for allowing every aspect of your life – the way you think and the way you act – to take on new depth and commitment. Discipline allows the sort of intellectual and moral clean-up that is required of us if we are to be faithful to our calling as Christians. It is our contribution to the God-given and grace-driven process of fitting us and enabling us to be the people of God in the world. It removes the obstacles to grace and renewal that clutter up our unredeemed lives.

Think of faith as being like a love affair. In all the best love affairs, you want to please the person you're in love with. It is a natural and perfectly understandable response to them. That means you will try to change the way you are, and to become what your loved one would like you to be. You start doing things you know they would like. Why? Because it's natural. That's what love is all about. It's not legalism, nor is it irrational. It is just part of the glorious business of being in love. Discipline in the Christian life is just our loving response to the love of God. It is our way of ensuring that we do not get in the way of God's task of reshaping and refashioning our lives. Discipline clears the decks of our spiritual lives, in order that God may deploy the full resources of his grace to renew us. And it is not inconsistent with the doctrine of justification by faith.

Justification by faith affirms that the Christian life does not begin through human achievement or merit, but as a gracious gift of God, on account of all that he has done for us through Jesus Christ. But that life, once started, needs to be continued – and part of that continuation is the process of sanctification, by which we are internally renewed by the work of the Holy Spirit. Discipline is our contribution, aided by God, to that process. We are not justified by discipline; but our sanctification is assisted by our willingness to collaborate with God, giving him breaks in our life, in order that we can become more like Christ.

Discipline in both personal and corporate life is thus the means by which the process of conforming to Christ may be facilitated. It is not something which one is being asked to undertake unaided; rather, it is a God-aided process of self-examination, by which obstacles to the goal of being conformed to Christ are identified – and dealt with. Discipline is seen as a form of spiritual obedience, a fruit of faith which itself can lead to new qualities of faith and commitment to God. For the reformers, an ill-disciplined army was useless when it came to a battle; similarly, ill-disciplined Christians have strictly limited value in the fight of faith. Although the military analogy may seem slightly offensive to some today, the basic point seems reliable: personal discipline makes a vital difference in personal relationships, the academic world, and the business world (to note just three examples). It can also make a vital difference to faith. To put it bluntly: disciplined faith is a faith which is likely to survive, and lead to faith in others.

The practical importance of this point is borne out by the fortunes of Calvinism in the Europe of the mid-sixteenth century.

Lutheranism generally spread and survived on account of the benign influence of local princes and monarchs, who found it congenial to their personal outlooks on life. Calvinism, however, had to survive and prosper under intensely hostile conditions. The case of France is instructive: from 1534 onwards, Calvinism was virtually a proscribed religion in that country. To be a Calvinist was to run the risk of rapidly (and unpleasantly) becoming a dead Calvinist. Yet Calvinism prospered. By the early 1560s, it looked as if Calvinism might end up becoming the dominant faith in that intensely hostile situation. How?

In part, the answer lies in the religious and economic attractiveness of Calvin's ideas, which did much to ensure they received a hearing. But the main part of that answer must lie in Calvin's insistence upon the need for his French followers to be disciplined. Small groups sprang up throughout the country, meeting regularly in secret to study the word of God, to pray, and to break bread together. Their survival depended upon the quality and resilience of their faith. There are fascinating parallels between these groups and the French resistance movements of the Second World War, such as the *Maquis* – not least because of the support given to them from a foreign country (Geneva). These sixteenth-century prototypes of small study groups proved to be the backbone of Calvinism in France. By developing regular patterns of prayer and Bible study, and by pledging their commitment to support each other in the event of difficulties, these groups developed faith of a quality which did much to ensure its future.

To conclude this chapter, we may take an image noted above, and develop it further. There are substantial parallels between French Calvinism and the French resistance during the Second World War. Both were fighting for their very existence in occupied territory. Their survival and their ultimate aims demanded faith and discipline. C.S. Lewis once compared the situation of modern Christians to resistance movements during that same war. Christians, he suggested, were living in occupied territory. The world has been taken over by a foreign power (an allusion to the forces often grouped together as 'sin, the world and the devil'). And Christians must lead the resistance struggle, until

the invading foreign power can be removed and the rightful
government restored (an allusion to God).

This image is helpful, not least on account of the severely
hostile nature of much modern western culture, which frequently seeks to portray Christianity and Christians as eccentric
hang-overs from a past age, and dismisses their concerns as
mere nostalgic hankering, reflecting an inability to cope with
change, or a misguided quest for certainty. But the point we
wish to make is this: survival depends upon personal discipline. Just as the endurance of those small groups of Calvinists
in sixteenth-century France depended upon discipline, so our
survival in the modern period may depend upon precisely that
same quality. The parallels are instructive – both between the
situations, and the means used to cope with them. We can learn
from those small groups in France, whom Calvin designated
églises plantées (planted churches), and their emphasis upon
discipline. As Calvin himself wrote, drawing upon a military
analogy: 'Christians must be prepared for the struggle which
God has ordained for all the godly. An armed enemy is at hand
– an enemy who is cunning and cannot be defeated by purely
human strength.' Discipline allows us to draw upon the strength
of God at such times. The college Christian Union Bible study,
the parish prayer meeting, the community fellowship group –
all are capable of acting as vital and disciplined cells, capable of
keeping faith going and growing under difficult circumstances.
And is this not central to the task of any spirituality?

Conclusion: Reformation Spirituality and the Modern Church

The reformers were not saints; they were just people who set out to enable the church to be faithful to its calling in the dangerous new world of the early modern period. We are heirs to that same calling and that same era of modern history. This book has argued that their outlooks, ideas and approaches can still be of use today. The resources of this classical Evangelical spirituality remain a living option for the modern church.

Time and time again, a cry goes out from Christian pastors and teachers. It could be summarised like this. We need a theology which meets the needs of the modern age. We need a spirituality which addresses the issues of a society ridden by guilt and fear. We need a gospel which will work in our cities. And yet it must be *Christian*. However relevant the approach may be, it must be authentic. Its Christian integrity must not be squandered, in favour of a transient network of beliefs, determined by our secular environment. Yet, as this work has stressed, we do not need to reinvent the wheel. The spirituality of the Reformation is an invaluable starting point and resource for renewing and refreshing a tired church, conscious of both its needs and its opportunities.

Ideas that work are rare – yet the aspects of Reformation spirituality that we have considered in this book have been tried and tested under the tough and demanding conditions of early modern Europe. Yet we need to reclaim and reappropriate them. Some of those ideas have become overlaid with dust and dirt; others have been abandoned, because they have been misunderstood. By making available those ideas, and stressing the importance of their historical context, this book has attempted to provide new resources and a new impetus to Christian living, in all its richness, in the modern period. This concluding chapter does not aim to summarise the contents of this work; it merely attempts to make some modest observations concerning the potential of such an approach to the needs of the modern church.

Reformation spirituality represents a challenge to return to the roots of our faith. It is an invitation to allow the past to interact with the present, to discover whether there are matters which we have suppressed or forgotten which ought to be recalled to memory and to use. The creative interplay of the traditional and the modern, which is a central feature of Reformation spirituality, can become ours as well. Traditionalism and modernism alike have their obvious defects, with one blind to the present and the other to the past. The modern period needs to be stimulated and nourished by the past, without being bound by its limitations.

For the past is not dead; it holds the key to our future. The Greek language possesses two words for time – *chronos* and *kairos*. The former (from which we derive such English words as chronometer and chronology) refers to the objective passage of time, to the ticking away of minutes, to the interval which separates us from ideas, events and people, and causes us to speak of them as being in the past. But time is also a subjective notion, something which cannot be defined purely in minutes, hours or years. There is a sense in which an idea is only old if we *feel* it to be old. The Greek word *kairos* relates to this aspect of time. It refers to a propitious moment in time, to a window of opportunity, when an idea or event (no matter what its *chronos*) breaks through the walls of our world and casts new and liberating light upon it.

As I have stressed throughout this work, the chronological age of ideas and values often gives little indication of their present-day relevance; that can only be tested in the laboratory of human experience. Many of the ideas linked with the Reformation have a surprisingly modern *feel* to them, despite their chronological age. Classical Evangelical spirituality is young at heart, with a long and distinguished future ahead of it – if we are prepared to use it and act upon it. It is like a seed, dormant but not dead, which has lain inactive for many years, but is capable of being reactivated and of growing.

Reformation Spirituality and the Individual

The early modern period may be said to represent the point in the history of the Christian church at which purely external understandings of Christianity came to be seen as irrelevant. Erasmus' *Handbook of the Christian Soldier* is a powerful witness to this development, stressing the need for an *internalised* understanding of the Christian faith. No longer was it adequate to define Christian faith and practice in purely external terms, such as attending church and receiving the sacraments. Instead, faith must be made relevant and real to the private experiential world of individuals. The subjective reality of faith became a popular issue, as it had never before.

The Reformation made a deliberate appeal to this new mood – and in doing so, believed it was not responding to some accident of history, but recovering a vital aspect of apostolic Christianity. Did not the writings of Paul show him to have been aware of the personal, subjective and experiential aspects of faith? Why, then, should not these insights and opportunities be made available to the whole people of God? The dawn of the early modern period was seen as a providential opportunity to retrieve lost or repressed aspects of authentic Christianity. Recovered Christianity was *real* Christianity.

The need to make the Christian faith relevant to individuals aware of their own subjectivity was a central feature of Reformation spirituality. To fail to make the gospel real to such people was potentially to write a theological suicide note. The world of medieval Christianity was dying – and there was every danger that Christianity might die with it, unless it could be restated and refashioned in ways related to the needs of the early modern person. The reformers gladly seized this nettle, believing that its flower was a priceless jewel. An historical development became the occasion for a long overdue restructuring of the faith. For to thus *refashion* Christianity was to *reform* Christianity – to restore it to its proper state, which would, it was passionately believed, prove relevant to the needs of this unknown new world. This enormously risky experiment proved successful. New methods of Bible study, preaching and teaching were devised, designed to explore and explain the enormous potential of the gospel to ordinary people.

This need still exists. There is still a danger that Christianity will be understood in external and formal terms as a set of practices. Those attitudes of the early modern period are still with us. The rise of existentialism is a powerful reminder of the continued need to relate the gospel to the subjective consciousness and experiential world of individuals. There is a continued need for what Kierkegaard called 'an appropriation process of the most passionate inwardness' (*Concluding Unscientific Postscript*). To fail to ground the gospel in the individual's world of experience is to risk compromising the future of Christianity itself.

This is not, however, to suggest that Christianity must be allowed to degenerate into the mists of a subjective individualism. The Reformation itself was careful to balance its stress upon the subjective aspects of faith with a firm emphasis upon the objective character of the Christian faith. Doctrine was seen as a vital corrective to the potential dangers of a concern with the subjective aspects of faith. Doctrine interprets experience; experience can never be allowed to be an authoritative source of truth in itself. As Luther's theology of the cross makes clear (pp. 73–80), the way things are experienced to be is not necessarily the way things actually are.

If the Reformation represents a considered rejection of a retreat into subjectivism, it extended the same critical approach to individualism. To develop this point, we may consider the role of the church in Reformation spirituality.

Reformation Spirituality and the Church

There is no way in which the Reformation endorsed radical Christian individualism. The insistence upon the need to make the Christian faith *relevant* to the individual was coupled with a stress upon the necessity to live the Christian life within the community of the church. The community of faith is not some accidental appendage to faith; the church is a God-given resource for the nurture of faith and spiritual growth. We are not meant to be 'lone rangers', but to walk with God in company with other Christians. There is a need for Evangelicals – the modern heirs of the Reformation – to recapture the corporate aspects of faith. Many modern Protestant writings, such as Dietrich Bonhoeffer's *Life Together*, have brought home the importance of a community in deepening personal and corporate faith and commitment.

Yet Reformation spirituality insisted that the vitality and potency of the institution of the church is directly linked to the quality of the commitment of its members. The effectiveness of the mission of the church cannot be isolated from the personal faith of its members. The Reformation ideal is that of a group of personally committed individuals, who choose to pool their commitment and talents to create a whole which is greater than the sum of its parts. Personal renewal and faith are essential components of the life of the church and, through it, of its impact upon society at large. In his famous study *The Monks of the West*, de Montalembert commented thus on St Benedict's impact on western society in the sixth century:

> Historians have vied in praising Benedict's genius and clear-sightedness; they have supposed that he intended to regenerate Europe, to stop the dissolution of society, to re-establish public education, and to preserve literature and the arts . . . I firmly believe that he never dreamt of regenerating anything but his own soul and those of his brethren, the monks.

Benedict illustrates a classic ideal of Evangelical spirituality – personal renewal undergirds institutional effectiveness and social action.

The institution of the church must thus never be allowed to eclipse personal faith, in that the former is sustained and strengthened by the latter, even if the former provides a safe and caring environment within which faith may grow. Faith in Christ must not become confused with a blind obedience to the institution of the church. Like all human institutions, the church is sinful and in need of reformation (a point stated pithily in the slogan *ecclesia semper reformanda*, 'the church must always be reforming itself'). To be a Christian is to be committed in the first place to God, and in the second to the institution of the church. And that commitment to the church must include a loving, caring criticism of that church, if it is to be faithful to its identity and calling.

The modern church, including modern Evangelicalism, still needs the kind of intellectual, moral and theological clean-up that Martin Luther sought for medieval Christendom. It needs a religious shake-up, in which it rediscovers its reason for being there, and its resources to enable it to recover and fulfil its calling. Just as the medieval church had – by accident rather than design – compromised the vitality of the gospel with all kinds of additions and distortions, so the modern church has cluttered up its faith with all kinds of ideas and attitudes of questionable value and dubious origins. There is a need for a shake-out. The Reformation offers us both a model and resources for such a refreshing correction. Purification may be painful – but it is also cleansing.

Refreshed by our Roots

A central theme of Reformation spirituality is that we need to return to our spiritual roots. We need to be surprised, nourished, challenged and informed by our past. Modern Evangelicalism has often unwittingly severed its connections with its identity-giving past. It has broken the bonds with its roots. It has largely lost sight of the enormous riches of its heritage, made available by the foundational thinkers of the sixteenth-century Reformation. This has had a number of alarming results. For example, much of modern Evangelicalism has retreated from the world into a narrow Christian subculture – a development which would have shocked and dismayed the reformers, who would have regarded it as intellectually shallow and theologically irresponsible.

Modern Evangelicalism urgently needs to rediscover the seminal ideas of the Reformation. It must be nourished and challenged by its roots, and look to the rock from which it was hewn. It needs to be *nourished*, in that it has been starved of serious intellectual and spiritual food. Half-understood secular ideas, loosely based upon self-help psychological manuals, have taken the place of serious engagement with Christian theology. And it needs to be *challenged*, in that it has often altogether evaded the biblically grounded ideas and attitudes forged by the reformers, substituting inadequate and inauthentic spiritualities largely incapable of meeting the needs of the modern situation. A sectarian mentality, dominated by the impulse to withdraw from the world, has come to dominate a movement which was originally committed to the conversion and transforma-tion of the world. Reconsidering the roots of Evangelicalism could be a powerful and overdue correction to this depressing development.

This book has been written in the conviction that the spiritu-ality of the Reformation has a continued contribution to make to the modern Christian church throughout the world. Statistic after statistic suggests that the forms of Christianity which are growing in the modern world are those which take their roots in Scripture and the Reformation tradition seriously. One of the greatest ironies of the twentieth century is that those churches which have sought to make the gospel more relevant to modern humanity by adopting modern ways of thinking, derived from secular culture, have seen their memberships decline dramati-cally. This search for relevance is commendable – but it has seriously miscarried.

Sadly, this quest for relevance lacked confidence in the innate ability of the Christian gospel to take care of itself. To be relevant is not to adopt the ideas of the world; it is to provide a viable, credible and attractive alternative to them. It is to have confidence in the gospel itself. Reformation spirituality, with its deep appeal to Scripture-nourished and Scripture-inspired roots, has much to offer the church in its search for a worldly relevance which is responsibly and authentically Christian. Classical Evangelical spirituality provides us with living options which relate to living issues.

Standing at the dawn of the early modern period, the reformers were obliged to address situations which bear a recognisable resemblance to our own. They forged biblically based spiritualities capable of meeting the needs and opportunities of their period. And, if we will allow them, they can be of use to us as well. Spirituality in the classic tradition has much to offer us, at times posing a challenge to the ways in which we think and act, and at others providing a valuable resource to complement existing approaches. In the midst of a blind and mindless rush to get on with the business of life, the Reformation invites us to pause and take stock of our situation, learning from the mistakes and successes of the past. This book is simply a modest attempt to allow the past to address and enrich the present.

But perhaps the central achievement of this classic Evangelical spirituality is its insistence, given expression in its doctrine of justification by faith, that we discover all over again that, today as yesterday, it is the wisdom and power of God, rather than what passes as their human equivalents, which sustain and nourish his church. Let Luther have the final word to that church, in bringing this book to an end:

> It is not we who can sustain the church, nor was it those who came before us, nor will it be those who come after us. It was, and is, and will be the one who says 'I am with you always, even to the end of time.' As it says in Hebrews 13: 'Jesus Christ, the same *yesterday, today* and *forever.*' And in Revelation 1: '*Who was*, and *is*, and *is to come.*' Truly, he is that one, and no one else is, or ever can be.
>
> For you and I were not alive thousands of years ago, yet the church was sustained without us – and it was done by the one of whom it says: '*Who was*' and '*Yesterday*' . . . The church would perish before our very eyes, and we along with it (as we demonstrate every day), if it were not for that other man who so obviously upholds the church and us. This we can lay hold of and feel, even if we are reluctant to believe it.

We must give ourselves to the one of whom it is said: '*Who is*' and '*Today*'.

Again, we can do nothing to sustain the church when we are dead. But he will do it, of whom it is said: '*Who is to come*', and '*For ever*'.

For Further Reading

There are surprisingly few works devoted specifically to the spirituality of the Reformation. The bibliography presented below is not exhaustive, and is restricted to the English language. It is intended to give the reader some idea of the resources available for further study of the issues raised in this book.

Works dealing with the history and thought of the Reformation:

Bainton, Roland H., *The Age of the Reformation* (Princeton, N.J.: Van Nostrand, 1956).
—, *Women of the Reformation* (3 vols. Minneapolis: Augsburg Publishing House, 1971–77).
—, *Here I Stand: A Life of Martin Luther* (Tring: Lion, 1987/ New York: Abingdon Press, 1950).
—, *Erasmus of Christendom* (Tring: Lion, 1988/ New York: Scribner, 1969).
Baker, Wayne J., *Heinrich Bullinger and the Covenant* (Athens, Ohio: Ohio University Press, 1980).
Battles, F.L., 'God Was Accommodating Himself to Human Capacity', *Interpretation* 31 (1977), pp. 19–38.
Bornkamm, Heinrich, *The Heart of Reformation Faith: The Fundamental Axioms of Evangelical Belief* (New York: Harper & Row, 1965).
—, *Luther in Mid-Career, 1521–30* (Philadelphia: Fortress Press, 1983).
Bouwsma, William J., *John Calvin: A Sixteenth-Century Portrait* (New York: Oxford University Press, 1988).

—, 'The Spirituality of John Calvin', in Jill Raitt (ed.), *Christian Spirituality II: High Middle Ages and Reformation*, (London: Routledge, 1987/ New York: Crossroad Publishing House, 1988), pp. 318–33.

Brecht, Martin, *Martin Luther: His Road to Reformation* (Philadelphia: Fortress Press, 1985).

Büsser, Fritz, 'The Spirituality of Zwingli and Bullinger', in Jill Raitt (ed.), *Christian Spirituality II:* (London: Routledge, 1987/ New York: Crossroad Publishing House, 1988), pp. 300–17.

Butler, Diana, 'God's Visible Glory: The Beauty of Nature in the Thought of John Calvin and Jonathan Edwards', *Westminster Theological Journal* 52 (1990), pp. 13–26.

Dillenberger, John, and Welch, Claude, *Protestant Christianity interpreted through its Development* (New York: Scribners, 1954).

Forde, Gerhard O., *Where God Meets Man: Luther's Down to Earth Approach to the Gospel* (Minneapolis: Augsburg Publishing House, 1972).

Ganoczy, Alexandre, *The Young Calvin* (Edinburgh: T. & T. Clark, 1988).

George, Timothy, *The Theology of the Reformers* (Nashville: Broadman Press, 1988).

Kittelson, James M., *Luther the Reformer: The Story of the Man and His Career* (Leicester: Inter-Varsity Press, 1989).

Leith, John H., *Calvin's Doctrine of the Christian Life* (Atlanta, Ga: John Knox/Westminster Press, 1989).

Lienhart, Marc, *Luther: Witness to Jesus Christ* (Minneapolis: Augsburg Publishing House, 1982).

von Loewenich, Walter, *Martin Luther: The Man and His Work* (Minneapolis: Augsburg Publishing House, 1986).

Lohse, Bernhard, *Martin Luther: An Introduction to His Life and Work* (Edinburgh: T. & T. Clark, 1987/Philadelphia: Fortress Press, 1986).

McGrath, Alister E., *Luther's Theology of the Cross: Martin Luther's Theological Breakthrough* (Oxford/Cambridge, Ma.: Basil Blackwell, 1985; reprinted 1990).

—, *The Intellectual Origins of the European Reformation* (Oxford/ Cambridge, Ma.: Basil Blackwell, 1987).

—, *Reformation Thought: An Introduction* (Oxford/Cambridge, Ma.: Basil Blackwell, 1988).

—, *A Life of John Calvin: A Study in the Shaping of Modern Western Culture* (Oxford/Cambridge, Ma.: Basil Blackwell, 1990).

McKee, Elsie Anne, and Armstrong, Brian G., *Probing the Reformed Tradition* (Louisville: Westminster/John Knox Press, 1989).

Maxcey, Carl E., *Bona Opera: A Study in the Development of the Doctrine in Philip Melanchthon* (Nieuwkoop: de Graaf, 1980).

Oberman, Heiko A., *Luther: Man Between God and the Devil* (New Haven: Yale University Press, 1989).

Parker, T.H.L., *John Calvin* (Tring: Lion, 1985).

Potter, G.R., *Zwingli* (Cambridge: Cambridge University Press, 1976).

Quere, Ralph Walter, *Melanchthon's Christum Cognoscere: Christ's Efficacious Presence in the Eucharistic Theology of Melanchthon* (Nieuwkoop: de Graaf, 1977).

Richard, Lucien Joseph, *The Spirituality of John Calvin* (Atlanta, Ga.: John Knox Press, 1974).

Schreiner, Susan, *Theater of His Glory: Nature and the Natural Order in the Thought of John Calvin* (Durham, NC: Labyrinth Press, 1990).

Spitz, Louis W., *The Protestant Reformation 1517–1559* (New York: Harper & Row, 1985).

Stauffer, Richard, *The Humanity of John Calvin* (Nashville: Abingdon Press, 1971).

Stephens, W.P., 'Zwingli's Reforming Ministry', *Expository Times* 93 (1981), pp. 6–10.

—, *The Theology of Huldrych Zwingli* (Oxford: Oxford University Press, 1986).

Tracy, James D., '*Ad Fontes*: The Humanist Understanding of Scripture as Nourishment for the Soul', in Jill Raitt, (ed.) *Christian Spirituality II: High Middle Ages and Reformation*, (London: Routledge, 1987/ New York: Crossroad Publishing House, 1988), pp. 252–67.

Wallace, Ronald S., *Calvin's Doctrine of the Christian Life* (Edinburgh: Oliver & Boyd, 1959).

Other works of interest and relevance:

Bonhoeffer, Dietrich, *Life Together* (London: SCM Press/ New York: Harper & Row, 1954).

Edwards, Tilden, *Spiritual Friend: Reclaiming the Gift of Spiritual Direction* (New York: Paulist Press, 1980).

Elton, G.R. (ed.), *The Reformation 1520–1559* (New Cambridge Modern History, Volume 2, 2nd edn: Cambridge University Press, 1990).

Forrester, W.R., *Christian Vocation* (New York: Scribners, 1953).

Foster, Richard J., *Celebration of Discipline* (London: Hodder & Stoughton 1989/ New York: Harper & Row, 1976).

Hunter, James Davison, *Evangelicalism: The Coming Generation* (Chicago: University of Chicago Press, 1987).

Kranzberg, Melvin, *By the Sweat of Thy Brow: Work in the Western World* (New York: Putnam, 1975/ London, Greenwood Press 1987).

Hendrik, Kraemer, *A Theology of the Laity* (Cambridge:Lutterworth Press/ Philadelphia: Westminster Press, 1958).

McGrath, Alister E., *Iustitia Dei: A History of the Christian Doctrine of Justification* (2 vols: Cambridge: Cambridge University Press, 1986).

Miles, Margaret R., *Practising Christianity: Critical Perspectives* (New York: Crossroad Publishing Company, 1988).

Nichols, J. Randall, *The Restoring Word: Preaching as Pastoral Communication* (San Francisco: Harper & Row, 1987).

Oden, Thomas C., *Care of Souls in the Classic Tradition* (Philadelphia: Fortress Press, 1984).

Simpson, Lewis, *The Dispossessed Garden: Pastoral and History in Southern Literature* (Athens, Ga.: University of Georgia Press, 1975).

Tilgher, Adriano, *Work* (New York: Arno Press, 1930).

Williams, Rowan, *The Wound of Knowledge: Christian Spirituality from the New Testament to St John of the Cross* (London: Darton, Longman & Todd, 1980).

Index

YOUR CONFIRMATION

John Stott

Your Confirmation has laid a firm foundation for the Christian faith in the lives of thousands since its first printing over thirty years ago. It is now completely rewritten for a new decade, and published in an attractive illustrated format.

As an introduction to the Christian faith, or as a refresher course in Christian fundamentals, *Your Confirmation* is invaluable, particularly with its new study guide and list of recommended reading.

The Rev Dr John R W Stott is a pastor, preacher, author and scholar known around the world. He is Rector Emeritus of All Souls Church, Langham Place, London.

THE MASTER

John Pollock

The extraordinary life and work of Christ is conveyed afresh in John Pollock's absorbing and acclaimed narrative. This international bestseller is now published in a brand new edition with full colour photographs.

'John Pollock has caught the sheer excitement of the events he records.'

Church Times

'May well become a modern classic.'

Billy Graham

The Rev John Pollock is Britain's foremost Christian biographer and has written about the lives of many notable church leaders in history, including Lord Shaftesbury and John Wesley.

JESUS: THE TRANSFORMING LEADER

Leighton Ford

In this new addition to the Jesus Library, Leighton Ford describes with great insight the leadership principles of Jesus, bringing Christians face to face with the challenge Jesus presents. 'He was able to create, articulate and communicate a compelling vision; to change what people talk about and dream of; to make his followers transcend self-interest; to enable us to see ourselves and our world in a new way; to provide prophetic insight into the very heart of things, and to bring about the highest order of change.'

LEIGHTON FORD is president of Leighton Ford Ministries which concentrates on the development of younger Christian leaders worldwide. An ordained Presbyterian minister, he served with Billy Graham for many years as an associate evangelist and vice president of the Billy Graham Association.

NEW TASKS FOR A RENEWED CHURCH

Tom Wright

The Christian Gospel is a radical one. It brings new life to individuals and challenges the very heart of society. Yet Western culture is increasingly secular and self-serving, hardly concerned with Christian truths. Has the Church's voice been silenced? Far from it, asserts Tom Wright. The Church is being renewed for the task that confronts it: combatting paganism with energy and conviction.

The Rev Dr Tom Wright is Fellow, Chaplain and Tutor in Theology at Worcester College, Oxford.